anythink

ROBERT E. LEE

Commander of the Confederate Army

ROBERT E. LEE

Commander of the Confederate Army

Mona Kerby

Enslow Publishers, Inc.
40 Industrial Road
Box 398
Berkeley Heights, NJ 07922
USA
http://www.enslow.com

To:

Robert H. Chambers, president and Joan Develin Coley,
provost of Western Maryland College

Copyright © 2015 by Mona Kerby

Originally published as *Robert E. Lee: Southern Hero of the Civil War* in 1997.

All rights reserved.

No part of this book may be reproduced by any means without the written permission of the publisher.

Library of Congress Cataloging-in-Publication Data

Kerby, Mona.
  Robert E. Lee : commander of the Confederate army / Mona Kerby.
    pages cm. — (Legendary American biographies)
  "Originally published as Robert E. Lee: Southern hero of the Civil War in 1997."
  Includes bibliographical references and index.
  ISBN 978-0-7660-6490-4
  1. Lee, Robert E. (Robert Edward), 1807-1870—Juvenile literature. 2. Generals—Confederate States of America—Biography—Juvenile literature. 3. Confederate States of America. Army—Biography—Juvenile literature. I. Title.
  E467.1.L4K47 2015
  973.7'3'092—dc23
  [B]
                                        2014031173

Future editions:
Paperback ISBN: 978-0-7660-6491-1
EPUB ISBN: 978-0-7660-6492-8
Single-User PDF ISBN: 978-0-7660-6493-5
Multi-User PDF ISBN: 978-0-7660-6494-2

Printed in the United States of America
102014 Bang Printing, Brainerd, Minn.
10 9 8 7 6 5 4 3 2 1

To Our Readers: We have done our best to make sure all internet addresses in this book were active and appropriate when we went to press. However, the author and the publisher have no control over and assume no liability for the material available on those internet sites or on other Web sites they may link to. Any comments or suggestions can be sent by e-mail to comments@enslow.com or to the address on the back cover.

✪ Enslow Publishers, Inc., is committed to printing our books on recycled paper. The paper in every book contains 10% to 30% post consumer waste (PCW). The cover board on the outside of each book contains 100% PCW. Our goal is to do our part to help young people and the environment too!

Photo Credits: Library of Congress, p. 6.

Cover Credit: Library of Congress

CONTENTS

Robert E. Lee

Chapter 1

A Tough Decision

On Saturday, December 23, 1860, Lieutenant Colonel Robert E. Lee arrived at Fort Mason, Texas, some one hundred miles northwest of San Antonio. On his journey by horseback from the Alamo city, a blue norther had blown in across the plains, chilling Lee to the bone and turning the landscape into an icy, slippery fairyland. At Fort Mason, Lee's officers and their families invited their fifty-three-year-old commander inside to join the Christmas party and to sit close by the fire. Robert E. Lee was welcomed.[1]

There was something about him that made him special. "To approach him," wrote Texan Rip Ford, "was to feel yourself in the presence of a man of superior intellect, possessing the capacity to accomplish great ends and the gift of controlling and leading men."[2] He was, wrote one Fort Mason soldier, "so calm, so serene, so thoughtful, and so commanding."[3]

Tall and handsome, Lee had steel-gray hair and penetrating brown eyes—eyes that seemed to express deep emotion. Children loved him.

On that Saturday night in December, Lee sat close to the fire, telling stories and making the children laugh. When the talk turned to the possibility of a civil war, Lee deflected the heated conversation by reminding them to have faith in God. As always, Lee kept his true feelings to himself.

No doubt, his thoughts turned toward home.[4] Some eighteen hundred miles away at Arlington House in Virginia, Mary Lee and their children were celebrating the holidays without him, again. This was not the first time Robert E. Lee had missed spending Christmas with his family. For thirty-one years, he had served as an officer in the United States Army. He had gone wherever duty called, which often meant leaving his family behind.

Far from home, Lee wrote letters to his wife and children. "Live in the world you inhabit," he wrote. "When a thing is done, we ought always make the best of it."[5] Most of the time, Robert Lee managed to do just that. But this Christmas, it was different. He was lonely.[6]

Perhaps Lee was tired of army life. At fifty-three, Lee's rheumatism bothered him, making his joints ache.[7]

Perhaps Lee was tired of Texas. The United States Army, with more soldiers stationed in Texas than any other place in the country, had yet to control Comanche attacks and raids from Mexican bandits.[8] Lee had already served as the colonel of the 2nd Cavalry from 1856 to 1858. In February 1860, he was back, serving as commander of the military department in Texas. It was, he wrote once, a "desert of dullness."[9] Some ten months later, in December 1860, he was relieved by General D. M. Twiggs. Still, Lee could not go home. Instead, he was ordered to Fort Mason, to his old command of the 2nd Cavalry.

Perhaps Lee was tired of traveling thousands of miles by horseback, tired of chasing Mexican bandits, tired of chasing the Comanches, tired of snakes and wolves, tired of worrying about the Army's unsuccessful use of camels instead of horses, tired of listening to boring court martials and writing up long reports, and tired of the Texas weather.[10]

He made the best of it, of course. As he watched the seasons pass in Texas, Lee described summer weddings in San Antonio held at midnight in order to escape the heat. He made light of the mosquitoes. Lee wrote to his wife, "I have a lively time within doors, the fleas by day and the mosketoes by night. I am so extremely awkward at catching them that they mock at my effort."[11]

But on that cold winter night of December 23, 1860, at an isolated post in Texas, if Lee was tired of Texas, or tired of army life, or lonely for his family, he kept those feelings to himself. It was his duty, after all.

It was his duty to wait. There was nothing much for Lee to do at that time. The Comanches were quiet. The newspapers that arrived from New Orleans talked of war. In a letter to his wife, Lee wrote, "As far as I can judge from the papers we are between a State of anarchy & Civil war."[12] The United States was embroiled in a state of lawlessness and political disorder. The news was bad, and Lee was far from home.

Slavery—was it a necessary evil? States' rights—did states have certain rights to decide issues for themselves instead of the federal government dictating what they should do? Should slavery be abolished by the federal government? It was the South against the North—geography played a role in the arguments. Most slaves lived in the South, where they worked on large plantations. White Southern plantation owners, with their gracious manners, did not appreciate "Yankees" telling them how to live. Reason was replaced by passion.

Already, South Carolina had seceded (formally withdrawn) from the United States of America. In January 1861, Mississippi, Florida, Alabama, Georgia, and Louisiana seceded as well. Soon, more states would follow.

Still, Lee waited, praying for peace. He wrote,

I wish to live under no other government, and there is no sacrifice I am not ready to make for the preservation of the Union save that of honour. If a disruption takes place, I shall go back in sorrow to my people and share the misery of my native state.[13]

Tensions mounted in Texas. Hot-headed Texans called for secession. Governor Sam Houston argued against it, but the Texans held a secession convention anyway, voting 167 to 7 to leave the Union. At the convention, women walked down the aisle and raised the Lone Star flag.

Sam Houston stood before a crowd full of hecklers, and though he silenced them with his words, his meaning escaped them.

Some of you laugh to scorn the idea of bloodshed as the result of secession, But let me tell you what is coming. Your fathers and husbands, your sons and brothers, will be herded at the point of the bayonet . . . You may, after the sacrifice of countless millions of treasure and hundreds of thousands of lives, as a bare possibility, win Southern independence . . . but I doubt it.[14]

Events rushed forward at a quickening pace. Robert E. Lee's time of waiting was over. At Fort Mason on February 13, 1861, he received an order to report immediately to General Winfield Scott in Washington, D.C. As Lee climbed into the wagon that would take him back to San Antonio, a captain asked, "Colonel, do you intend to go South or remain North?"[15]

"I shall never bear arms against the United States—but it may be necessary for me to carry a musket in defense of my native state, Virginia," Lee replied.

The driver cracked the whip, and they were off. Lee turned around and shouted, "Good-by! God bless you!"[16]

Three days later, when Lee arrived in San Antonio, he found the city in turmoil. That morning, General Twiggs had relinquished his command of the United States Army to the Confederates. Soldiers guarded the streets. The plaza near the Alamo looked like a "military camp."[17] "Has it come so soon to this," asked Lee.[18]

On March 1, Lee arrived home in Virginia. When he reported to General Scott's office in Washington, D.C., the two friends talked for hours. Even though both men were Virginians, Scott's first allegiance was to the United States of America. Scott hoped to persuade Lee to accept command of the powerful Union Army, hoping that a superior army led by Lee could end a civil war quickly.[19] On March 28, Lee was given the permanent rank of colonel in the United States Army. His papers were signed by Abraham Lincoln. Lee accepted.

Events began to boil. More Southern states seceded from the Union, and even though they claimed to believe in the individual rights of states, they hurriedly formed a new country, the Confederate States of America. On April 14, 1861, the United States Army surrendered Fort Sumter to the Confederates. There was no turning back.

President Lincoln called for seventy-five thousand soldiers. On April 17, 1861, a secession convention was held in Virginia. Would Virginia secede from the Union? On that same day, both General Scott and Francis P. Blair, a close friend of President Lincoln, asked Lee to come to Washington for a meeting.

Lee went. Scott and Blair talked to Lee separately. Accept command of the Union Army, they urged. They believed that if Lee would take command of the greatest army on earth, the war would soon be over.

How would Lee answer, a man whose wife was the daughter of the adopted son of George Washington, the father of the United States of America? How would Lee answer, a man who loved his state of Virginia, yet did not own a single acre of land? How would Lee answer, a man who had written in 1856 that "slavery as an institution, is a moral & political evil?"[20] How would Lee answer, a man who believed in doing his duty?

Who was Robert E. Lee, and why did his answer change American history?

Chapter 2

He "Carried the Keys"

He was a Virginian. Though it is never fair to sum up a person with one word, perhaps the word Virginian best describes Robert Edward Lee. In those years, people were extremely loyal to their native state, and they sometimes felt more loyalty to their state than to their country. Virginians, however, were especially loyal to both. After all, a Virginian—George Washington—was the first president of the United States and the father of our country.

To be sure, Lee was very much his mother's son. He loved Ann Carter Lee and followed her example of self-denial and self-control to the end of his life. He never really knew his father; even so, the escapades of Light-Horse Harry Lee marked him. But just as important as his family, it was his place, his geography that shaped Lee. Love of country, Virginia, family—these characteristics marked proud Virginians. These were characteristics of Robert Edward Lee.

Family

Both of Lee's parents were Virginians. His mother, Ann Carter Lee, was a descendant of "King" Carter, a wealthy Virginian. His father, Henry Lee III, nicknamed Light-Horse Harry, was the governor of Virginia. He was also a hero in the American Revolution. An excellent horseman, Light-Horse Harry led his men on daring raids. George Washington praised him.

Ann Carter Lee was seventeen years younger than her husband and was his second wife. His first wife had died. Still, on June 18, 1793, when the couple married, it seemed like a wonderful match. The *Virginia Gazette* reported that the wedding "promises the most auspicious fortune . . ."[1] Even George Washington wrote to Light-Horse Harry, sending his blessings to the couple.

Ann Carter Lee and Light-Horse Harry would need all the blessings they could get, because instead of fortune, the couple faced financial disaster. Light-Horse Harry may have been a war hero, but he was not good with money. He would often borrow money and buy land, hoping to sell it quickly for a large profit. When the big profits did not materialize, he would sell the land and be in debt. Unfortunately, Light-Horse Harry kept repeating his mistakes. He even borrowed money from his father and from George Washington and did not pay either of them back.

Once, according to rumor, Light-Horse Harry asked to borrow a horse from a neighbor. The neighbor agreed and sent along a slave to bring the horse home. Weeks went by before the slave returned and reported that Light-Horse Harry had sold the horse. "Why didn't you come home?" his master asked. "Cause," the slave replied, "General Lee sold me, too."[2]

Right before his marriage to Ann Carter, Light-Horse Harry tried to mend his ways and do something he was good at—soldiering. He asked to be the commander of the United

States Army, but George Washington refused his request. Light-Horse Harry was a good soldier, explained Washington, but "lacks economy."[3] In response, Light-Horse Harry said that he would go to France and join the army. But Washington reminded him that he was still the governor of Virginia. Light-Horse Harry stayed home.

If Ann Carter Lee had been blind to Light-Horse Harry's faults on her wedding day, she recognized them soon enough.[4] Family meant everything to her, however, and she was determined to make the best of her situation. She was, after all, a Virginian.

It was not easy. In the years between 1793 and 1802, Ann Carter Lee gave birth four times. She lost the first baby, but the other three children survived—Charles Carter, born in 1798; Ann, born in 1800; and Sidney Smith, born in 1802. For a while, they lived at Stratford Hall in the Northern Neck of Virginia. The estate had belonged to Light-Horse Harry's first wife, and she had willed it to their firstborn son, because she knew that her husband was not good with money. In debt, Light-Horse Harry sold off the furniture and portions of the estate, neither of which belonged to him. To save on heating expenses, the Lees lived in just a few rooms on the first floor.

Birth

In 1806, Ann was pregnant again. Her father died that year, so she took her children and went home for several months to her family's plantation, the Shirley Estate on the James River. That December, Ann asked Light-Horse Harry to send a carriage for her, but he had sold that, too. Ann and her children had to return to Stratford in a carriage without a top. Ann caught a cold.

On January 19, 1807, in spite of her sickness, Ann gave birth to a healthy son. She named him Robert Edward, after two of her favorite brothers. It is said that Robert was born in the same room as Richard Henry Lee and Francis Lightfoot Lee, two ancestors who had both signed the Declaration of Independence.[5] No one knows if Light-Horse Harry was present for the birth.

However, it is known where he was two years later—in jail. In 1809, when he could not pay his debts, Light-Horse Harry was ordered to spend several nights in a courthouse cell. Ann and the children remained at Stratford Hall. In 1810, when Light-Horse Harry was released, the family moved to Alexandria, Virginia.

In Alexandria, there were plenty of Carters and Lees to turn to whenever Ann needed help. Relatives lived right next door and just down the street. Cut across one cousin's garden and there was the house of another relative. Since the Lees could not afford to own their own house, Ann and the children lived with various relatives. In 1811, another daughter, Mildred, was born to the Lees.

In the summer of 1812, when Robert was five, America declared war against Great Britain. Light-Horse Harry was in Baltimore, Maryland. He was ambivalent about the War of 1812, but when an angry mob attacked one of his friends because he was against the war, Light-Horse Harry defended him. He landed in jail, again. The mob stormed the jail and the bloody fight continued. Someone poured hot candle wax in Light-Horse Harry's eyes. Another man tried to cut off his nose. They left him for dead. Light-Horse Harry lived, but he never really recovered.

In 1813, when Robert was six, his father sailed for Barbados. No longer governor of Virginia, Light-Horse Harry was sick and broke. He promised to return in good health and with money. He did neither. His wife supported him as best as she could on what little money her father had left her.

Light-Horse Harry was a better soldier than provider, but this does not mean that he did not love his family or that they did not love him. In Barbados, he wrote long, loving letters to Ann and to his son, Charles Carter Lee, who was called Carter. Carter was nine years older than Robert. In one letter to Carter, his father wrote, "Robert was always good, and will be confirmed in his happy turn of mind by his ever-watchful and affectionate mother. Does he strengthen his native tendency?"[6]

George Washington's Eulogy

When George Washington died, Congress asked Light-Horse Harry Lee to write the eulogy, the speech praising the president. He coined the phrase that later became famous, "First in war, first in peace, and first in the hearts of his countrymen."[7]

This letter has been reprinted in countless biographies on Robert E. Lee. Light-Horse Harry Lee, for all of his faults, left his son Robert a legacy more valuable than money: He told the world that his son was good.

In March 1818, the old war hero was on his way home when he became very sick. His ship landed in Georgia so that Light-Horse Harry could get medical care, but he died two weeks later.

Perhaps Light-Horse Harry influenced Robert in a more subtle, yet powerful way. His own life served as an example of how not to live. Years later, when Robert E. Lee was an old man, he edited his father's war memoirs. He did not mention his father's debts or the years his father spent in jail. But he knew.

Ann Carter Lee had taught Robert well. Love your family. Practice self-control. Think of others instead of yourself. Do not spend money foolishly.[8] She taught him to take pride in himself and in his home state, Virginia.

Early Years

Not much is known about Robert as a very young boy. There is a family story about three-year-old Robert saying good-bye to the iron angels in the fireplace at Stratford Hall.[9] There is another family story about young Robert going visiting with his mother and crawling under his friend's crib to go to sleep.[10] His half-brother Henry once described Robert looking "sheepish and shamefaced" when he had lost a tooth.[11] For some reason, Robert wanted to hide the missing tooth from his brother so he scrunched up his face and would not look at him.

Robert found plenty to do growing up in Alexandria. It was a thriving town of seventy-five hundred people. There were 260 shops, 34 taverns, a library, and water wells at the end of the streets. At night, the watchmen came along and lit the oil lamps on the corners. In loud voices, they called out the time and the weather. While it was against the law to fly kites or play ball in the streets, there was always something to do in the meadow nearby.[12]

Robert liked to hunt because he liked to run after the hounds all day long.[13] There were many cousins to play with and to visit. In fact, there were so many cousins, they even had school together. The girls usually had school at the Shirley plantation, and the boys had school at Eastern View in Fauquier County, Virginia.[14] As Carter explained, "we had a large family circle."[15]

Robert was a good child. By the time he was eleven, his father was dead and his brother Carter was away in school at Harvard. His other brother, Sidney Smith Lee, had joined the Navy. Robert's older sister Ann was not well, and Mildred was still very young. Their mother, Ann Carter Lee, was in poor health. She probably had tuberculosis, a disease that affected her lungs. The only person who could care for her was Robert, and he did.

He enrolled in classes at Alexandria Academy. Before and after school, Robert was the family's housekeeper. He did the shopping. He also did the outside chores and cared for his mother's horses. While other boys played, Robert bundled his mother up and took her for drives in the carriage, and made her laugh. At thirteen, Robert had full responsibility for the house and servants. As people used to say in those days, he "carried the keys."[16]

When he grew up, Robert Lee explained countless times that he "owed everything" to his mother.[17] By her example, he had learned to be careful with money, to think of others before himself, and to love. Love of country, of Virginia, of family—Ann Carter Lee had taught him well. Robert E. Lee was a Virginian through and through.

Chapter 3

THE "MARBLE MODEL"

In 1824, the world marched forward. In New York, the Erie Canal opened for business. In Texas, Stephen F. Austin and three hundred American colonists had just settled new land and were trying to live peacefully with the Mexican government. In Germany, Beethoven, who was by then totally deaf, completed his Symphony #9 in D Major.

But in Virginia, Robert Lee was not thinking about historical events. Instead, he was thinking about his future.

Tall and handsome, with a wave in his dark hair that young girls liked, the seventeen-year-old had finished three years at the Alexandria Academy, where he had been an excellent student. He could quote Greek and Latin, and he was especially good at math. People said he was "bright, animated, and charming" and a "youth of great promise."[1]

However, the "youth of great promise" did not have a penny to his name. If Robert Lee wanted to have any kind of a career, he was going to have to get a college education—cheap.

By February 1824, his family had settled on a plan. They would try to get Robert an appointment to West Point Military Academy in New York. His father had been a good soldier, and just maybe Robert would be a good one, too. He could study engineering, a field that required math, one of his favorite subjects. At West Point, Robert would get a college education in return for serving one year in the Army, and it would not cost him a penny.[2]

Robert E. Lee's family and friends started sending letters to Secretary of War John C. Calhoun, who made the appointments to West Point.[3] Robert's brother Carter Lee wrote a letter, and so did his half-brother Henry Lee. One friend of the family wrote that Robert "is the son of Gen. Henry Lee [who has a] strong claim to the gratitude of his country." Furthermore, the friend declared, Robert's mother was "one of the finest women, the State of Virginia has ever produced."[4]

Robert's teacher, William B. Leary, verified that Robert was a good student. "[W]hen examined," Leary wrote, "he will neither disappoint me or his friends."[5] Another friend mentioned Robert's "excellent disposition."[6] Virginia Congressman C. F. Mercer wrote a letter on Robert's behalf and then had it signed by five senators and three representatives.

Robert and his friends and family had done everything in their power to get him admitted to West Point. There was nothing else to do but wait.

In March 1824, Robert received the official decision from the War Department. The family objective had been achieved—Robert was appointed to West Point. Because there were so many appointments that year, however, Robert would have to wait until July 1825. But that was okay. Robert's future was decided. He was going to be an engineer and a soldier.

On April 1, 1824, Robert E. Lee formally accepted the appointment. "I hereby accept the appointment . . . which I have been honnoured. . . ." he wrote, misspelling the word.[7]

That fall, the Marquis de Lafayette, the French general who had fought in the American Revolution, came back to the United States for a visit. On October 14, 1824, he stopped in Alexandria, Virginia, so that he could pay his respects to the widow of one of his American friends—Light-Horse Harry Lee.

During the visit, if Lee had any dreams about the glory of war, he kept them to himself. If he was going to succeed at West Point, he would have to prepare, and in the winter of 1825, that's exactly what he did.

Lee began an intense study of mathematics. His teacher claimed that Lee was a "most exemplary pupil in every respect." Lee drew complicated geometric figures using chalk and a slate with care—as if they were to be "engraved and printed" instead of being erased. Lee was good at *finishing up.*"[8]

Ann Carter Lee had reason to be proud of her children. But they were growing up and leaving home. "How can I live without Robert?" she asked. "He is both son and daughter to me."[9]

In June 1825, it was time for eighteen-year-old Robert E. Lee to begin his career.

United States Military Academy, West Point, New York

Lee traveled alone by train to New York City, where he booked passage on a steamboat. For thirty-seven miles, the steamboat churned up the Hudson River. It stopped at a large point of land jutting out from the western side of the river. The land rose straight up, some 190 feet above the river, and flattened out to a large plain studded with rows of tents. This was Camp Adams at the United States Military Academy at West Point, New York.

On that summer day in 1825, Lee surveyed his surroundings. If he had doubts about his decision to come to West Point, he did not mention them. His mother had taught Lee to practice self-control and pay attention to detail. These lessons were about to come in handy.

Cadets were ordered to buy a mirror, wash basin, stand, pitcher, pail, broom, and a scrub brush. They were ordered to buy their uniforms—dress grays, fatigue blues, four pairs of white summer pants, high-top shoes, and a hat—and, oh, what a hat it was. Made out of black leather, it had a shiny brim and was seven inches tall with an eight-inch-long plume. The heavy contraption strapped under the chin and was hot to wear.[10]

The cadets bought their uniforms and supplies out of their pay, which they had not yet earned. Pay was sixteen dollars a month and allowance was an additional twelve dollars. The cadets were in debt immediately.

Day after day, Lee and the other cadets marched up and down the plain. They marched in the heat and rain. At night, they slept in tents. When they were not marching, they were tested orally on their school subjects. Twenty cadets failed the academic tests and were sent home. Robert passed and stayed.

That fall, life at West Point did not get much easier. The cadets moved into the barracks. There were three or four cadets to a room. At night, they unrolled thin mattresses and slept on the floor. Cadets washed by using their basins and a bucket of cold water.

At West Point, the food was terrible. For breakfast, the cadets ate boiled meat, boiled potatoes, bread, and butter. For lunch, they ate boiled meat, boiled potatoes, bread, and butter. For supper, they ate bread and butter. Occasionally, they had something different, but it was not necessarily better. Cockroaches floated in the soup. One cadet dug into his bread pudding and discovered three tiny mice.[11]

Every waking minute of the cadets' day was planned. At 5:30 in the morning, a gunshot announced the new day, whereby the cadets dressed and raced outside for roll call. Classes, study, meals, marching, and recreation were all rigidly scheduled until 10:00 at night when taps sounded. The only free times were Sunday afternoons, Christmas Day, and New Year's Day.

There were rules against just about everything. It was against the rules to read novels, have visitors, or leave without permission. It was against the rules to drink, play cards, play games, and to have cooking utensils. Fist fights, of course, were also against the rules.

Cadets received a certain number of demerits (points off) for breaking the rules. Some cadets broke rules just by making simple mistakes. Other cadets broke the rules deliberately. More than one cadet slipped out at night and headed for Benny's Tavern. When William T. Sherman, later a famous Union general in the Civil War, was at West Point, he stole a chicken and cooked it in his room.[12]

Lee's Looks

During his life, people often commented on Robert E. Lee's good looks. One of the West Point cadets said that Lee's "personal appearance surpassed in manly beauty that of any cadet" and noted that his excellent posture "had none of the stiffness so often assumed by men who affect to be very strict in their ideas of what is military."[13]

Lee stood at five feet eleven inches, tall for that time. He had a big chest, big hands, and uncommonly tiny feet. His shoe size was 4½C.[14]

So, how did Robert E. Lee fare in such an environment? In a word—terrific. Lee did not break the rules. He was a good soldier and a good student. He was even good-looking. One cadet remarked that Lee was so handsome and well proportioned that he looked as if he had been sculpted. In fact, the cadets called him the "Marble Model."[15]

After two years, in the summer of 1827, Lee received permission to go home for a brief visit. Smith and Carter were there, and the three brothers attended one party after another. They must have turned more than one girl's head. Carter was considered the fun-loving one; Smith was the best-looking one, and Robert was the most dignified. One girl said that Robert Lee had "lovely manners," and that he was "as full of life, fun, and particularly of teasing, as any of us."[16]

In the fall, Lee was back at West Point. For the next two years, he studied mathematics, French, drawing, engineering, how to organize armies, how to give battle orders, and all about artillery. During one semester he checked out fifty-three library books, and one of them was written by his father. He stayed away from novels, however. They were, after all, against the rules.

In his last year, Lee received the highest award given to a cadet. Because of his excellent grades and military skills, he was named adjutant of the corps. When he graduated in June 1829, Lee was second in his class. In the four years that he was at West Point, he had not earned a single demerit. This was an extremely unusual accomplishment.

Robert Lee would spend the next year in the Army, but for now, it was time for the "Marble Model" to go home. His mother needed him.

Chapter 4

DUTY AND FAMILY

Ann Carter Lee was dying. For years, she had been sick, and at fifty-six, she could not hold out any longer. In June of 1829, twenty-two-year-old Robert Lee arrived home and nursed his mother, one last time. If he left the room, his mother "kept her eyes on the door till he returned."[1]

How she must have loved her handsome son, with the dark wavy hair and the penetrating brown eyes. Shy around people he did not know, Lee never gave a long speech in his entire life.[2] Somehow his eyes seemed to express what he left unspoken. Surely Ann Carter Lee must have looked at her son and accepted his love. She died on July 26, 1829.

For the next few months, Lee stayed with family and friends. But this was nothing new to him. As a result of Light-Horse Harry's debts, Ann and her children had been at the mercy of others. They were always guests, never staying in one place for too long.

Occasionally, Lee called on Mary Custis. On starry nights, as the young couple strolled in Mary's rose garden, Lee no doubt dreamed of the future. If he dreamed of wonderful places the Army would send him, those dreams were dashed soon enough. The Army ordered him to a swamp. Cockspur Island sat in the middle of the Savannah River, twelve miles south of Savannah, Georgia. It was hot, humid, marshy, and it had sand fleas that bit. In November 1829, Lee—not one for being late—arrived two weeks early.[3]

As an engineer for the Army, Lee was assigned to begin a foundation for a fort. He worked in mud up to his armpits, building dikes, ditches, and a dock. In his spare time, he wrote to Mary Custis. When he could visit Savannah, he enjoyed seeing Jim MacKay, a friend from West Point. Lee often teased and flirted with Jim's sisters.

But when it came to marriage, Lee—always the Virginian— chose a wife from a prominent Virginian family. In the summer of 1830, he went home to Virginia and, over a piece of fruitcake, asked Mary Custis to marry him.[4] She was not as pretty as he was handsome, but that did not matter.[5] They decided to marry the following summer.

In a way, it was a better match for Lee than it was for Custis. While the Lee name was respected enough in Virginia, his fiancée was from one of the most respected families in the entire country. Her father, George Washington Parke Custis, was the adopted son of George Washington.

Mr. Custis was a short, balding man with a big belly who loved to call himself the "child of Mount Vernon."[6] Somewhat eccentric, he enjoyed showing off Washington's possessions—his books, his clothes, his bed.

Custis had built a mansion, which he named Arlington House. It looked like a Greek temple with columns, and it stood on a thousand-acre plantation, overlooking the Potomac River and the United States Capitol. Inside, the dreary rooms were unpleasant and messy. To Custis, it was always more important to impress with outward appearances.

After spending the summer in Virginia, Lee returned to Cockspur Island. Storms had destroyed everything he had built, so he started over. The site eventually became Fort Pulaski, but Lee never worked on the actual fort. In May 1831, the Army reassigned him to Fort Monroe, Virginia, and ordered him to build a moat.

This would be the pattern for his entire career in the Army. Lee would start a project and then be reassigned before the work was completed—frustrating for a person who enjoyed "finishing up."[7] In the beginning of his career, Lee occasionally said he wanted to quit the Army, yet as he grew older, his letters reflected a change. He began to emphasize that he must do his duty.[8]

Marriage

On June 30, 1831, Robert Lee and Mary Custis married at Arlington House. On that rainy evening, as the young couple stood before the preacher, Lee was so nervous that he claimed he was as "bold as a sheep."[9]

Afterward, of course, there was laughing, talking, and celebrating. They laughed about the preacher, who had arrived soaking wet and who had to wear a pair of Mr. Custis's pants. Mr. Custis was short and fat; the preacher was tall and skinny. As the night went on, everything got a little livelier because Mr. Custis had spiked the punch with alcohol. The punchbowl had a ship painted on it, and Mr. Custis told the men they had to keep drinking until they came to the hull. After that, Mr. Custis invited everyone to spend the night, as long as they did not mind sleeping three to a bed.[10]

To other people, and perhaps to Lee himself, his wedding seemed a way of continuing the legacy of George Washington and honoring the characteristics that Virginians held dear. "This marriage," wrote one of Lee's relatives, "in the eyes of the world, made Robert Lee the representative of the family of the founder of American liberty."[11]

Wedded bliss became reality soon enough. At Fort Monroe, the couple lived in two small rooms. Slaves took care of the cooking and cleaning. Even so, Mrs. Lee distinguished herself as messy, lazy, forgetful, and almost constantly tardy. Lee, on the other hand, was neat, orderly, and punctual. Once, he explained to guests, "Tell the ladies that . . . Mrs. L. is somewhat addicted to *laziness & forgetfulness* in her housekeeping . . . in her mother's words, 'The spirit is willing but the flesh is weak.'"[12]

Mrs. Lee had a streak of evangelical religious zeal that Lee did not share. Lee believed in controlling emotions, not in expressing them dramatically. However, it is hard to find a letter of Lee's in which he does not mention praying or doing the right thing. Although he regularly attended church—occasionally falling asleep during long sermons—he did not join a congregation until late in life. For whatever reasons, Mrs. Lee prayed for her husband's soul.[13]

Mrs. Lee missed her mother, and since she could pray for her husband's soul anyplace, she went home—to her mother and to Arlington House.[14]

Mrs. Lee did not move home permanently, of course. She and her husband loved one another, but she stayed at home a lot. Mary remained at Arlington House for various reasons, such as when she was having a baby or perhaps just because Arlington House was so much more pleasant than army quarters.

Lee missed his wife, and one time he tried to make her jealous, hoping that she would leave her mother and come to him. He wrote to his wife about escorting a certain lady to visit another lady. "Think of that Mrs. Lee," he wrote, "How I did strut along."[15]

But Mrs. Lee did not seem to mind. Perhaps it was because she did not feel well. She was a small, frail woman, and she did not have a lot of energy, especially after her children were born. In 1832, their first child, George Washington Custis Lee, nicknamed "Boo," was born. In 1835, their daughter Mary Custis, called "Daughter," was born, and Mrs. Lee took a turn for the worse. This time, it was she who begged her husband to come. Lee, who had been sent to Detroit, Michigan, by the Army, refused, explaining that he must perform his "duty."[16]

In all, they had seven children. Following Boo and Daughter, William Henry Fitzhugh, "Rooney," was born in 1837. Anne, "Annie," was born in 1839. Agnes, "Wigs," was born in 1841. Robert Edward, Jr., "Rob," was born in 1843, and Mildred, "Precious Life," was born in 1846. Mrs. Lee began to suffer from arthritis, which eventually crippled her.

Lee's Ideas About Parenting

In a letter from Louisville, Kentucky, dated June 5, 1839, Lee wrote to his wife:

> *You do not know how much I have missed you and the children, my dear Mary. To be alone in a crowd is very solitary . . . If I could only get a squeeze at that little fellow turning up his sweet mouth to "keese Baba"! You must . . . exercise firm authority over all of them. This will not require severity, or even strictness, but constant attention and an unwavering course.*[17]

After Fort Monroe, Lee spent four years in St. Louis, Missouri, on the Mississippi River. His family was with him some of the time. Lee's task was to change the course of the river, and he actually figured out a way to do it. But once again, the Army transferred him before the project was finished. In 1838, he was promoted to captain. From 1840–1846, Captain Lee worked as an engineer at Fort Hamilton in Brooklyn, New York.

While Lee was away from his family, he read parenting books, and in his letters home, he warned his wife not to be too lenient. He wrote his children, telling them to be good.[18] During his years in New York, a black-and-white terrier named Spec kept him company.

Lee also enjoyed the company of women. He enjoyed light-hearted conversations and regularly wrote to several women friends. He called the wife of a friend, "my beautiful Talcott."[19] In 1844, he began writing to eighteen-year-old Martha Custis "Markie" Williams, one of Mrs. Lee's relatives, whom he wrote to faithfully until he died. "You are right in my interest in the pretty women," Lee wrote a friend in 1845.[20]

Still, these were friendships only. Lee remained faithful to his wife. Mrs. Lee knew that her husband had women friends, and apparently she understood that the friendships would remain just that. She never appeared to be jealous.[21]

In 1846, Lee was thirty-nine years old. Careful with money, he had managed to accumulate some wealth. Lee had served in a peace-time Army, doing his job, doing his duty. But he was not yet a hero.

George Washington had been a war hero, and so had Light-Horse Harry Lee. How could Robert E. Lee uphold the family tradition? How could he leave his own mark on the world? In 1846, when the United States declared war on Mexico, Lee decided what he must do.

Lee, the Army engineer, asked to go to war.

Chapter 5

Moving Toward War

In 1846, the United States declared war on Mexico. The United States government wanted land that belonged to Mexico—land that eventually became California, Nevada, Utah, New Mexico, and Arizona. They also wanted to extend the Texas border to the Rio Grande River. President James Knox Polk offered money, but the Mexican government ignored the offer. When a minor fight occurred on the Texas border, the United States quickly declared war. By February 1848, it was over. The United States got the land they wanted at a cheaper price than they had originally offered. In the process, thousands of Americans were killed, and the United States lost the goodwill of the Mexican government.

It was an unpopular war for many reasons. It was the first time that Americans had ever fought on foreign soil, and many Americans did not like to think of themselves as aggressors. Also, the Mexican War was viewed by some Americans as a way to extend slavery. Already, slavery was a heated political debate, dividing the North and the South. Most Southern plantation owners favored slavery because they needed laborers to work in the fields. (This was before mechanical farm machines had been invented.) The North, with more industry, was not dependent on slave labor.

Lee, who always believed in controlling his emotions, stayed out of the political debate. He saw the Mexican War as a way to further his career, and that is exactly what he did. During the war, he was promoted to lieutenant colonel, and then to brevet (temporary) colonel.

At the beginning of the war, Lee used his engineering skills to help build a flying bridge, a temporary bridge over the Rio Grande at Eagle Pass. Because the Army needed maps, the engineers took over reconnaissance work. They surveyed the land, made maps, and pointed out ways to use the terrain to their advantage in battle.

As a staff officer under General Winfield Scott, Lee was terrific at reconnaissance. He was good at figuring out how to cross difficult terrain and attack the enemy forces. At Cerro Gordo, Lee found a route through the mountains that allowed the Americans to attack Mexican General Antonio López de Santa Anna's army on its left flank. The surprise attack caught the Mexicans off guard, and the Americans won the battle. Santa Anna later said that "he had not believed a goat could have approached in that direction."[1]

At Pedregal, the Americans encountered a gigantic volcanic lava bed, with sharp rocks, steep ridges, and deep cracks that made it nearly impossible for the Army to cross. Yet, during the night, Lee discovered a route. At the fortress of Chapultepec, high on top a rocky plain, Lee planned a way to successfully storm the hill. Lee was wounded, but the injury was not serious.

Lee was brave. He did not get sick, did not need much sleep, and could ride hundreds of miles by horseback. General Scott called him the "gallant and indefatigable Captain Lee."[2]

By serving as an advisor on General Scott's staff, Lee learned how to make war and how a smaller force could successfully attack a larger one. He learned how to take chances and attack, how to flank an army, and he learned the importance of reconnaissance. Robert E. Lee, said General Scott, was the "very best soldier I ever saw in the field."[3] He was, Scott claimed, a "military genius."[4]

In some of his letters home, Lee was dark and brooding. To his son Custis, he wrote, "You have no idea what a horrible sight a battlefield is."[5] To his mother-in-law, he wrote, "I have done no good."[6] Lee had learned something about himself—he was good at something terrible. He was good at war.

After the Mexican War

On June 29, 1848, after being away from home for almost two years, Lee rode up to Arlington House on horseback. Spec the dog was the only one who recognized him. His children stared at him, noticing the gray in his hair and the wrinkles on his face. Lee called out, "Where is my little boy?"[7] Then, he stretched out his arms and embraced the neighbor's child.

Years later, Lee's son Rob wrote that their father "was always bright and gay with us little folk, romping, playing, and joking with us." In the early mornings, Lee loved to gather the children into bed with him, talking to them in "his bright, entertaining way." In the evenings, Lee enjoyed telling stories while his children tickled his feet. If they forgot, he would say, "No tickling, no story!" A family friend noted that "everybody and everything—his family, his friends, his horse, and his dog—loves Colonel Lee."[8]

From 1849 to 1852, Lee worked in Baltimore, once again doing engineering work for the Army, this time at Soller's Point. Mrs. Lee and the children divided their time between Baltimore and Arlington. Mary Custis Lee never liked being gone from Arlington House too long.

In 1852, the Army assigned Lee to be the Superintendent of the United States Military Academy at West Point, and he obeyed with "reluctance."[9] Never caring for politics or politicians, Lee did not look forward to being in charge of decisions in such a "snake pit," as he called it.[10]

While he was superintendent, he was able to make a few building improvements and a few changes in discipline, but he did not get the Army to adopt a more comfortable cap—the cadets were still wearing the same style that Lee had worn as a cadet. Occasionally, West Point's rules and regulations complicated ordinary events. For example, when one mother wanted to send her son some underwear, she first had to ask Lee, who then had to ask permission from Jefferson Davis, the secretary of war.[11]

James Whistler

Cadet James Whistler had to receive permission from the secretary of war before his mother could send him underwear. Later, Whistler was dismissed from West Point for having failed a chemistry test and for having excessive demerits. This was probably for the best. He went on to become a famous American painter. His mother's portrait, formally named Arrangement in Grey and Black, *became better known as* Whistler's Mother.

During these years, the Lee family was together much of the time. Lee's son Custis attended West Point, graduating first in his class in 1854. Lee's nephew, Fitzhugh Lee, Smith's son, also attended West Point. Lee was especially fond of Cadet James Ewell Brown (J.E.B.) Stuart. (Later, Stuart would serve in the Virginia Cavalry under Lee.) In 1853, Mrs. Lee's mother died, and she went home for an extended visit.

In 1855, Lee was forty-eight years old. He had spent some twenty-five years in the Army, and although he had served as an advisor during the Mexican War, he had never been in charge of troops. When Secretary of War Davis appointed Lee to the rank of lieutenant colonel of the United States 2nd Cavalry, Lee eagerly accepted. There was one condition. The post was in Texas.

Lee left his family at Arlington House, and in March 1856, he arrived in San Antonio, Texas. By horseback, he headed for Camp Cooper, located at a fork of the Brazos River. The 2nd Cavalry had the responsibility of protecting settlers from Comanche attacks. Lee patrolled hundreds of desolate miles, and while he never had to fight the Comanches, he wrote his wife that "these people give a world of trouble to man and horse, and poor creatures, they are not worth it."[12]

When he was not out on patrol, Lee attended court-martial trials. One case was on the Rio Grande, which was seven hundred miles away from Camp Cooper. It took him twenty-seven days to get there.[13] Texas was a wild, desolate country, and Lee began to think that God must be punishing him.[14]

In 1857, his father-in-law died, and Lee went home for what he thought was a two-month furlough. When he arrived, he found that his wife was nearly crippled with arthritis. Lee also discovered that he had been left with the responsibility of putting his father-in-law's messy affairs in order. Lee received a leave and stayed two years.

Mr. Custis owed ten thousand dollars on unpaid bills. He had been rich in land but poor in money. He owned three farms but had neglected their upkeep. Buildings needed painting. Roofs needed repair. Fields needed plowing. The will stated that Lee's three sons were to receive farms and that his four daughters were to receive ten thousand dollars each. Somehow, Lee was supposed to get the farms in good shape and then find the forty thousand dollars for his daughters' inheritances. After that, according to the confusing will, Lee was supposed to free Mr. Custis's slaves within five years.

Lee was not one of those Southerners who believed wholeheartedly in slavery. Yet he did not agree with abolitionists who wanted to immediately free slaves. Lee felt that many black people were not smart enough to take care of themselves.[15] Lee, always one for controlling emotions, believed that angry abolitionists just stirred up trouble. Still, in 1856, he had written to his wife that "slavery as an institution, is a moral & political evil."[16]

However, confronted with his father-in-law's will, Lee put Mr. Custis's slaves to work, hoping to pay off some of his father-in-law's debts. When the *New York Tribune* heard about it, they attacked Lee in the paper, calling him a cruel slave owner.

Agnes Lee's Diary

In 1852, Agnes Lee, the eleven-year-old daughter of Robert E. Lee, began a diary that she kept for five years. She recorded daily life at West Point, including her observations of the cadets on the school campus, at church, and at dinner parties at their home. Published for the first time in 1984, it was titled: Growing Up in the 1850s: The Journal of Agnes Lee.

Lee, the gracious Virginian, did not reply. Still, he wrote to his son Custis. Your grandfather, he said, "has left me an unpleasant legacy."[17]

On October 17, 1859, Lee was working at Arlington when J.E.B. Stuart, the former West Point cadet, rode up with a message. Lee was needed in Washington, D.C., immediately. Lee left right away, not even pausing to change his clothes.

John Brown, an abolitionist who violently opposed slavery, had led a small group of men in an attack on Harpers Ferry, located in the western part of Virginia, where the Potomac and Shenandoah Rivers meet. Brown's men stormed the arsenal, which held the government's supply of guns and ammunition. They intended to arm the slaves and start a rebellion. Lee was put in charge of United States forces and was sent to stop Brown.

At ten o'clock that night, Lee and the soldiers arrived by train at Harpers Ferry. The attackers had locked themselves and some captives in the firehouse. Lee studied the situation and came up with a plan.

Early the next morning, the United States troops surrounded the firehouse. A company of United States Marines prepared for attack, holding sledgehammers and bayonets. Their guns were not loaded, however. Lee did not want to harm the captives. Under a white flag, Stuart went to the firehouse. When Brown opened the door, Stuart read aloud a note from Lee, demanding that the attackers surrender immediately. If they did not, the note read, Lee could not guarantee their safety. Brown shut the door.

The Marines charged, but the door held fast. The Marines grabbed a ladder and rammed the door, making a hole. Their lieutenant crawled inside and attacked Brown, slashing his neck slightly with his sword. Again, the lieutenant struck, but his sword hit something hard—Brown's belt buckle perhaps—and bent in half. Brown did not die.

Even so, the battle was over in three minutes. Two of Brown's men were killed, but the captives were unharmed. Robert E. Lee's plan had worked.

John Brown was tried in court, charged with treason, and hanged. It was a sensational trial, covered by the major newspapers, and it stirred up ugly debates. Some Northerners hailed Brown as a hero and a saint. Most white Southerners hated Brown fiercely.

Lee was sent back to Texas. He went back to long days in the saddle, boring court trials, and missing his family in Virginia. He would not return until summoned by General Winfield Scott.

Some said John Brown was a madman. Maybe he was and maybe he wasn't. But he knew, as did Robert E. Lee, that slavery was evil. Brown's hanging added fuel to the emotional fire. The country was one step closer to civil war.

Chapter 6

"THE DIRTIEST
MEN I EVER SAW"

Y es and no are such easy words, yet sometimes they are the hardest words to say. Robert E. Lee was asked to answer either yes or no. His answer changed his life, the lives of his family, and the lives of millions of Americans—forever.

On April 17, 1861, in Washington, D.C., Lee met first with Francis P. Blair, a friend of the president, and then with General Winfield Scott. On behalf of President Abraham Lincoln, Blair offered Lee the command of the entire United States Army. General Scott knew that Lee was perhaps the best officer in the Army. He encouraged Lee to accept command.

In 1861, few people would have predicted that the Civil War would last four years. Few would have predicted that more than six hundred thousand Americans would die, more than in any other war the United States has ever fought.

The country was in turmoil. Calm reasoning had evaporated, and passions reigned supreme. Northern abolitionists cried for an end to slavery. Southern political leaders threatened to secede—leave the Union—if the United States government did not recognize states' rights. In fact, South Carolina had seceded soon after President Lincoln was elected. They feared that Lincoln would abolish slavery, even though the president had made no such promises. The arguments over states' rights and slavery pitted the North against the South, friend against friend, brother against brother, and soldier against soldier.

Faced with a possible war between the states, soldiers and officers in the United States Army had to decide. Should they fight for their country, which they had pledged to do, or should they resign and fight for their native state? General Winfield Scott, a Virginian, had already made his choice. He would be loyal to his country. What would Robert E. Lee decide?

After meeting with Blair and Scott, Lee rode home to Arlington House. There, he wrestled with the most difficult decision of his life. Lee was a proud Virginian, yet he did not own a single acre of Virginia soil. He owned slaves, but he did not wholeheartedly support slavery. He agreed that states had certain rights, but he did not believe in secession. For over thirty years, Robert Lee had faithfully served in the United States Army.

Virginia, duty, family—the significance of these words had been instilled in Lee as a boy, and they defined him as a man. On April 20, 1861, Robert E. Lee resigned from the United States Army. His answer to his country was no.

On that same day, Lee wrote to his sister in Baltimore. He knew that Ann would remain loyal to the Union, and he tried to explain his reasons. "I have not been able to make up my mind to raise my hand against my relatives, my children, my home," he wrote. "I know you will blame me; but you must think as kindly of me as you can, and believe that I have endeavored to do what I thought right."[1]

General Scott told Lee, "You have made the greatest mistake of your life."[2]

Virginia soon seceded from the Union and joined the new Southern nation, the Confederate States of America. On April 22, 1861, Lee accepted command of the military and naval forces of Virginia. This was strictly an advisory position. Still, to the Virginians, Lee "appeared every inch a soldier and a man born to command," and they cheered.[3] Lee, however, was in no mood to celebrate war.

But he would do his duty for Virginia. Within weeks, Lee had mobilized an army. The South's economy was based on agriculture, and because there was little manufacturing, the Confederacy could produce neither guns nor uniforms. Lee managed to round up forty-six thousand guns in Virginia, but many of the guns were old muskets left over from the Revolutionary War. The soldiers had to provide their own uniforms.[4] The cavalry also had to provide their own horses.

The industrialized United States never had these manufacturing problems. The Union Army provided uniforms for all its soldiers and supplied them with over a million guns.[5]

By May 1861, the Union forces had invaded northern Virginia and seized Arlington House. Soldiers ransacked Lee's home, destroying the furniture and chopping down trees. Mrs. Lee fled, leaving behind the cat. In Lee's letters to her, he joked about the cat and the "Yankees," trying to ease her grief. Mrs. Lee refused his comfort. The Union soldiers had stolen her home, and she hated them for the rest of her life.

During the first year of the war, Lee advised Confederate President Jefferson Davis. He offered battle strategies and organized forces, but he did not lead the war against the United States. Eventually, the role of advisor became more and more frustrating for Lee.

When he arrived in western Virginia in August 1861, the weather was wet and bitterly cold. The Confederate Army was disorganized, but when Lee offered suggestions, he was ignored.

When the Confederate Army failed to attack the Union Army on Cheat Mountain, the Southern newspapers blamed Lee and called him "Granny Lee."[6]

Lee ignored the insults and continued to do his best, his duty. After three months in western Virginia, Lee was promoted to full general. He grew a beard. He also found the best horse he had ever owned. Lee named the horse Traveller.

In November 1861, President Davis ordered Lee to defend the coastline of South Carolina, Georgia, and Florida from a Union attack. Because men and guns were in short supply, this was nearly an impossible task. But Lee was an expert at organization, and in three months time, he managed to increase the coastal fortification.

Richmond, Virginia, 1862

In March 1862, President Davis ordered Lee to Richmond, Virginia. This was the seat of the Confederate capital and government. Lee, still an advisor, was charged with organizing the Confederate Army. The Confederacy was in trouble.

Traveller

Robert E. Lee loved all horses, but his favorite was a gray stallion named Traveller. Big, strong, and spirited, he was first named Jeff Davis, then Greenbriar. When Lee bought him, he renamed him Traveller because he traveled so well. Lee and Traveller were together throughout the Civil War—from western Virginia in 1861 to Appomattox, Virginia, in 1865.

According to Lee, Traveller "would inspire a poet." He endured "toil, hunger, thirst, heat, cold, and . . . dangers" and he responded "to every wish of his rider." After Lee's death, Traveller died from lockjaw, after stepping on a nail.[7]

In one battle after another, the Confederates had been defeated. The Southern soldiers, having signed up for one year, were ready to quit and go home. The Union Army outnumbered them in every way. The Union had more equipment, more guns, and more men. That spring, they had one hundred thousand soldiers marching toward Richmond. Disaster was in the air.

Lee pushed for the Conscription Act, which allowed the Confederacy to draft soldiers. Southern men between the ages of eighteen and forty-five were ordered to the battlefront. Some ten thousand Confederate soldiers arrived to defend Richmond, but because there were no extra guns available, Lee sent pikes (spears).[8]

Lee's sons, Custis and Rooney, were already serving the Confederacy. Custis worked on President Davis's staff, and Rooney was in the cavalry. The year before, Lee had refused to give his son Rob permission, saying that he was too young. Now that the Southern cause looked like it was about to fail, Lee allowed nineteen-year-old Rob to enlist.

Lee asked General Thomas J. "Stonewall" Jackson to take the offensive in the Shenandoah Valley in Virginia, and to prevent the Union from joining the march on Richmond. Jackson faced a superior army. But he was an aggressive fighter, an expert at strategy, and a hero to his men. Stonewall—who loved the Lord and war—started pushing. He rallied his forces and prepared to fight.

Tensions mounted as Union General George McClellan and his one hundred thousand soldiers started marching toward Richmond. Women and children began to leave the city. Confederate General Joseph E. Johnston prepared to defend Richmond, but his men were outnumbered two to one. "Our enemies are pressing us everywhere," Lee wrote.[9]

By May 1862, Lee was losing everything he had tried to protect. His savings were diminished. His sons were at war, and all of their property, which they had inherited from their grandfather, was in enemy hands. Even Mrs. Lee was behind enemy lines. She had ignored her husband's pleas to get to safety. Mrs. Lee was taken to General McClellan's headquarters. He treated Mrs. Lee kindly—"a courtesy she did not return"—and saw that she was safely escorted to Richmond.[10]

With his staff, Lee continued to be cheerful and pleasant, but these things were on his mind when President Davis called a cabinet meeting on May 9, 1862. We must, said Davis, evacuate the capital.

The room hushed. Later, one of the men remarked that he had never before seen such emotion on Lee's face. Lee had lost his possessions, but he had one thing left—his duty to Virginia—and this, he refused to relinquish. Lee's voice filled the room. "Richmond must not be given up," he said.[11]

Richmond was not evacuated.

On May 31, 1862, Johnston attacked the Union Army at the Battle of Seven Pines/Fair Oaks, Virginia, and was severely wounded. The day-long battle had powerful consequences for the Confederates. President Davis replaced Johnston and put Lee in command.

Commanding General of the Army of Northern Virginia

On June 1, 1862, Commanding General Robert E. Lee ordered the Army of Northern Virginia to dig, to pick up their shovels and fortify their position. The men grumbled and called their new commander "King of Spades."[12]

For days, Lee planned and plotted. He had one advantage— he knew McClellan's fighting style. During the Mexican War, Lee and McClellan had worked together on military strategies. Lee knew that McClellan, while good at organizing armies, hesitated to fight. Lee was about to play McClellan like a chess game. Backed into a corner and faced with an army twice the size of his own, Lee came up with a strategy: attack and wipe out McClellan's army. Lee's plan was to engage the enemy in battle. He would get the enemy to fire on Richmond. Then, the Confederate Army would launch a surprise attack on the enemy's right flank.

The battle started on June 25, and for seven days, the two armies fought in Virginia at Oak Grove, Mechanicsville, Savage Station, and White Oak Swamp. On July 1, the seventh day, they fought at Malvern Hill. Still outmanned and outgunned, Lee saw that his right flank attack was not going to work, but he refused to surrender.

Take the hill, Lee ordered Confederate General D. H. Hill, and take it head-on. The Confederates were slaughtered. "It was not war," Hill said later, "it was murder."[13]

Yet, on the eighth day, the Union Army had had enough. It turned around and retreated. While Lee did not wipe out McClellan's forces, he had put a larger and superior army on the run.

Many things had gone wrong during the seven-day battle. Lee had made mistakes in judgment. Some of the subordinate generals had not obeyed his orders; Lee had them reassigned elsewhere. Lee kept Jackson, however, even though he had been late for every battle. Later on, this proved to be a good decision when together they successfully planned the Union defeat at Chancellorsville, Virginia. Lee kept General James Longstreet, who was always slow to fight unless he was satisfied with his position, but once he started, he would not quit. "My old warhorse," Lee called him.[14] Lee also kept J.E.B. Stuart. Stuart, the brave and sometimes reckless commander of the cavalry, would be the "eyes" of Lee's army.

After the Battle of Seven Days, soldiers and newspaper editors stopped calling Lee "Granny Lee" or "King of Spades."

Instead, they started calling him a hero, for McClellan and his superior army completely withdrew from Richmond. The great Union attack had failed.

They had not seen anything yet. During August 28 through 30, 1862, at what became known as the Second Battle of Manassas (called the Second Battle of Bull Run in the North), the Confederate Army met the Union Army led by General John Pope. Lee used every stream, every woods, every hill to his advantage. Even though he faced a larger army, Robert divided his own army in half, a daring move to make.

On the afternoon of August 30, the air echoed with the high-pitched scream of the "Rebel yell." Longstreet's men hit the Union Army on its flank, while Jackson's men rushed forward. The Union did not stand a chance. At sunset, they started retreating. Once again, Lee had shown his genius for winning at war.

Mary Chestnut's View of Lee

Southerner Mary Chestnut, whose husband served as an aide to the Confederate President Jefferson Davis, kept a diary, rich in details about the Civil War and the Confederacy. She had this to say about Robert E. Lee and his brother Smith Lee. "All the same, I like Smith Lee better . . . Can anybody say they know his brother? I doubt it. He looks so cold and quiet and grand."[15]

The victory had taken a toll on Lee's soldiers, however. Stragglers were leaving the army without permission. Most of the soldiers had not eaten in three days. Their clothes were in rags, and thousands of them did not have shoes. Lee was injured. He had been standing beside Traveller when someone yelled. Traveller reared up, and Lee grabbed for the reins, missed, and fell down, severely spraining both hands and breaking one of his bones. But neither hunger nor hardship would stop the Army of Northern Virginia. Lee declared that the army "cannot afford to be idle."[16] They headed toward Maryland.

Invasion of Maryland

There were several reasons for Lee's decision to invade central Maryland. First, if Maryland were "freed" from the North, then perhaps her citizens would fight for the Southern cause. Second, if Lee could beat the enemy, then perhaps the United States would accept a peace proposal and recognize the independence of the Confederacy. Third, and most importantly, if it worked, the war would be over.

In September 1862, some forty thousand Confederates crossed the Potomac River and headed toward Frederick, Maryland. "They were the dirtiest men I ever saw," one boy remembered. "Yet there was a dash about them that the Northern men lacked."[17]

They would need that dash. Some seventy-five thousand Union soldiers were waiting for them in Frederick. As usual, the Union soldiers outnumbered the Confederates by the thousands. As usual, this did not stop Lee. His plan was even bolder than the one before. On September 9, he wrote out Special Orders No. 191.

Lee divided his army and sent them off in four different directions. The plan was risky. McClellan could easily overpower such small numbers of men, one group at time, but Lee knew that McClellan moved cautiously and slowly.

Jackson memorized Special Orders No. 191 rather than carry it around. Longstreet read his copy, then tore it into pieces and chewed it up. One unnamed staff officer decided to keep a copy as a souvenir. He wrapped it around three cigars and put it in his pocket. This was a mistake.[18]

On September 13, near Frederick, two Union soldiers found the cigars and the lost orders. Within hours, George McClellan knew Lee's plan. McClellan had everything he needed to win.

On September 14, at Turner's and Crampton's Gaps in South Mountain, the Union forces attacked the Confederates and overpowered them. Lee had no choice. Withdraw, he ordered. Go west through Sharpsburg, Maryland.

Yet for some unknown reason, McClellan, who could have wiped them out, waited.

On the morning of September 15, Jackson sent word that he was on his way from Harpers Ferry. Lee looked at the land surrounding the village of Sharpsburg and at the hills west of Antietam Creek. He stopped the withdrawal, deciding to fight there.

The Battle of Sharpsburg, known as the Battle of Antietam in the North, began at dawn on September 17, 1862. Fighting was fierce. In one brief lull, Rob saw his father. "General, are you going to send us in again?" "Yes, my son," Lee replied, and he smiled.[19]

The armies fought at East Wood, in the cornfield, West Wood, Dunker Church, and Bloody Lane. At the last possible moment, A. P. Hill's men arrived and managed to save the Army of Northern Virginia.

When darkness finally fell, lanterns dotted the fighting fields as medics searched for the wounded. By the end of the day, some ten thousand Confederate soldiers were dead or wounded. The Union suffered twelve thousand casualties. It was one of the bloodiest battles of the war.

During the night of September 18, Lee ordered his army to begin the long march home. McClellan's army did not follow. Because Lee retreated, McClellan claimed victory, but neither side really won.

In the fall of 1862, United States President Abraham Lincoln replaced General George McClellan with Ambrose Burnside. Lincoln needed a general who would fight aggressively. Lee feared that such changes would continue "till they find some one whom I don't understand."[20]

That fall, President Lincoln also announced that he would issue the Emancipation Proclamation on January 1, 1863, which would declare all slaves in rebellious sections to be free. Now, the North was not merely suppressing a rebellion. They were fighting for noble reasons. They were fighting to preserve the Union and to end slavery.

Also that fall, Lee's twenty-four-year-old daughter Annie caught typhoid fever and died. Lee learned of her death while reading his letters. On the morning the news arrived, Lee said nothing. He and his assistant, Walter Taylor, worked together, and Lee never showed any emotion. Later, however, when Taylor returned unannounced, he found Lee "overcome with grief."[21] For Lee, duty would always come first.

Fredericksburg, Virginia

In December 1862, Lee's army dug in and waited along Marye's Heights in Fredericksburg, Virginia. On December 13, Union soldiers commanded by General Burnside ran across open ground, uphill toward Marye's Heights. They were easy targets. Lee's army slaughtered them. Lee watched.

What did he say—this polite, courtly Virginian who believed in duty and honor, who smiled as he sent his son into battle, and who cried in private for his dead daughter? He said what you would expect him to say, a man who was very good at something terrible.

"It is well that war is so terrible," said Lee. "We should grow too fond of it."[22]

Chapter 7

"WHERE IS MY CAVALRY?"

The winter of 1862–63 was cold, rainy, and muddy. After the Battle of Fredericksburg, the Union Army retreated north, crossing the Rappahannock River. Burnside's attempted return lapsed into an impossible "Mud March." For the rest of the winter, the Union Army camped across the river, while the Confederate Army settled down in Fredericksburg.

Morale should have been low among the soldiers in the Army of Northern Virginia. They were cold and hungry. Each man's daily rations consisted of a quarter-pound of bacon (usually spoiled) and eighteen ounces of cornmeal that included the ground-up cob. Every third day, ten men shared one pound of rice.[1] While some Confederate soldiers had been issued uniforms—made of a rough weave gray-colored cotton that bleached out into a butternut color—many wore their own clothes, and these were in tatters. More than one "Butternut" had stolen a blue coat and boots off a dead Union soldier. One Confederate was taking a soldier's boot when the wounded man moved and looked at him. "Beg pardon, sir," said the Confederate, "I thought you had gone above."[2] In spite of everything that winter, the Army of Northern Virginia laughed a lot.

Perhaps morale was high because of the men's faith in Lee. His fairness to them, his simplicity, and his extraordinary ability to conquer a larger army had made him their hero. Perhaps they were devoted to Lee because he gave them the credit for his victories. "There never were such men in an army before," he said. "They will go anywhere and do anything if properly led."[3]

Lee spent Christmas at Fredericksburg, sleeping in his tent and getting caught up on paperwork. On December 29, 1862, Lee freed his father-in-law's slaves as his will had demanded—two days before President Lincoln's Emancipation Proclamation went into effect.

In the winter and early spring of 1863, Lee was ill, with what he said was a bad cold. The fifty-six-year-old general took to bed. "Old age & sorrow is wearing me away," he wrote to his wife.[4] By early April, he was able to work a little. This was good, because Union General Joseph "Fighting Joe" Hooker was on his way.

Hooker, who had replaced Burnside as the commanding general of the Army of the Potomac, was very sure of himself. "My plans are perfect," he boasted. "May God have mercy on Bobby Lee; for I shall have none."[5]

By April 27, 1863, the Union Army had crossed the Rappahannock and was heading west in an attempt to cut off the Confederates' supplies. Two big yellow balloons floated above carrying Union soldiers who were keeping an eye on the Confederates. Hooker had some one hundred thirty thousand men; Lee had sixty thousand. The odds were greatly in Hooker's favor.

Since Lee was not sure where Hooker would attack, he kept some troops at Fredericksburg and sent others west toward Chancellorsville, Virginia. The Confederates positioned themselves between the Orange Turnpike and the Orange Plank Road in an area called the Wilderness. The Wilderness—a thick tangle of trees, scrub oak, brambles, and vines—could tear off a person's clothes.

The Battle of Chancellorsville started on May 1, but that afternoon, for unexplained reasons, Hooker ordered a withdrawal. His actions disgusted his generals and puzzled Lee.

Lee met with Jackson, and the two men sat on a log among some pine trees and talked. Stuart rode up and announced that Hooker's flank was completely unprotected. Jackson and Lee agreed on a daring plan.

Jackson and twenty-six thousand men would march west, hoping to surprise Hooker's army and strike them from the rear. This meant that only ten thousand men would be left to defend Fredericksburg, and Lee would have only seventeen thousand men to attack Chancellorsville. It was a gamble. Lee took the chance.

About five o'clock on May 2, Union soldiers had just stacked their guns and sat down to supper, when deer and rabbit sprang from the Wilderness. The Union soldiers laughed. Then, in an instant, their looks changed to horror as Jackson's men came scrambling out of the Wilderness, yelling that fiendish Rebel yell. The Union Army disintegrated into mass confusion and retreat.

While surveying the front, Jackson was accidentally shot by his own men. A. P. Hill was also hit. Stuart was now temporarily in charge. Lee refused to hear the details of Jackson's injuries; he had no time for emotion.

On May 3, the Confederates attacked at dawn. Stuart attacked from the west. Lee attacked from the east and south. The Confederate artillery, well positioned at Hazel Grove, southwest of Chancellorsville, fired away. At 9:00 A.M., Hooker was standing on a house porch when an artillery ball struck and split a porch column, and the column hit him. His men laid him on a blanket. Hooker insisted on getting on his horse, and as he did, another ball hit the blanket where he had just been lying. Dazed, Hooker headed for the rear of his army.

The woods were in flames. The air was white with gun smoke. As Lee and Traveller rode into Chancellorsville, the soldiers—those still standing and those lying wounded on the ground—cheered for Lee. The Army of Northern Virginia had won, again.

The Battle of Chancellorsville was the greatest battle of Lee's career. Though the odds had been against him, he had boldly attacked. Lee had put still another Union general on the run.

However, the glory was fleeting. Union General John Sedgwick had taken Fredericksburg. On May 4, Lee counterattacked, but so soon after Chancellorsville, his subordinate generals could not carry out his plans. Fredericksburg remained in Union hands.

Still, the rest of Hooker's army was already retreating across the Rappahannock River. Hooker's perfect plans had been spoiled by Bobby Lee.

Lee never saw Jackson again. Surgeons amputated Stonewall Jackson's left arm. "He has lost his left arm," said Lee, "but I have lost my right."[6] On May 10, 1863, Thomas J. "Stonewall" Jackson died.

Jackson's Last Words

Right before Jackson died, it seemed as if he were reliving a battle. "Order A. P. Hill to prepare for action!" he called. He paused, then he smiled and said, "Let us cross over the river and rest under the shade of the trees."[7]

Flushed with victory, Lee was not about to quit. In less than a month, the Army of Northern Virginia was on the move. We must, said Lee, invade Pennsylvania and take the war to the enemy.

Gettysburg, Pennsylvania

As Lee explained, the soldiers and horses needed food, and they could get food north of the Potomac River, where the war had not destroyed the fields and crops. Second, and most importantly, Lee wanted a major battle—a final battle—to end the war and to establish independence for the Confederacy. Short on men and supplies and always fighting a superior army, Lee would have to strike soon and surprise the Union Army, or else he would not be able to win. "If God gives us the victory," said Lee, "the war will be over."[8]

Lee sent Stuart and his cavalry to keep an eye on the Union Army. On June 17, Lee joined the march with his men, hoping to keep his own army's whereabouts a secret from the enemy.

As the Confederate soldiers marched northward, the rolling farmland of Maryland and southern Pennsylvania delighted them. One Texas private wrote home saying that the barns were "positively more tastily built than two thirds of the houses in Waco."[9] There was plenty of food. Lee ordered his men to pay for what they took. They paid with Confederate scrip—money that was useless to Union farmers.

The Marylanders gawked at Lee. He was so dignified and handsome. In Hagerstown, a Union girl saw Lee and exclaimed, "Oh, how I wish he was ours." When some of the people commented on Lee's large neck, one Confederate replied that Lee needed that big neck to hold his head.[10]

On June 28, 1863, the Confederate Army stopped west of South Mountain, near Chambersburg, Pennsylvania. Stuart was missing, and this meant that Lee did not know the position of the

Union Army. The situation was serious. He could not continue without knowing the position of the enemy. Lee asked repeatedly, "Where on earth is my cavalry?"[11]

Stuart had been detained. First, his cavalry skirmished with some Union cavalry. Then, at Rockville, Maryland, Stuart captured a Union supply-wagon train, which slowed him down even more. When Stuart finally made it to Pennsylvania, he could not find the Army of Northern Virginia. Good excuses to be sure, but Stuart's actions had left Lee blind on enemy soil.

Near midnight on June 28, a spy named Henry T. Harrison arrived with information. With Stuart missing, Lee took a chance on Harrison. The Union Army, said Harrison, was south of the Confederates and moving toward them. What's more, Hooker had been replaced by Union General George Meade, the fourth Union general to go against Lee. So far, none of them had managed to beat Lee. His staff laughed about Meade, thinking that he would be no better than the others. Lee was not so sure. Lee had intended to surprise the Union Army. Instead, they had surprised him.

Unknown to Lee, on the morning of June 30, Confederate James Pettigrew's brigade marched down the Chambersburg Pike into Gettysburg, Pennsylvania. The men were after supplies. (One version of the story is that they wanted shoes.) When they spotted Union cavalry coming from the south on Emmitsburg Road and heading their way, they quickly retreated. But the Confederates wanted those supplies, and early on the morning of July 1, they headed back to Gettysburg.

John Buford and the Union cavalry were waiting. Positioned along McPherson's Ridge, north and south of the Chambersburg Pike, Buford's cavalry was small. "The devil's to pay," muttered Buford.[12]

The battle was on.

For six hours, the two sides fought, and Lee knew nothing about it. Frustrated that he had not heard from Stuart, Lee decided to ride into Gettysburg to see if he could get some news. At two o'clock in the afternoon, Lee heard the sound of artillery. Once again, Lee was surprised.

Before he could order a withdrawal, his army roared to life. It flanked the Union forces and pushed them east and south of Gettysburg. The Union soldiers scrambled up Cemetery Hill.

Lee studied the land. The high ground formed the shape of a fish hook, or a backward question mark. Big Round Top was the dot of the question mark, followed by Little Round Top. Cemetery Ridge was the shaft. Cemetery Hill was at the curve of the hill, followed by Culp's Hill. The backward question mark—fishhook—stretched four miles long.[13]

The best ground for fighting was the high ground. By 4:30 P.M., Meade's Union Army was beginning to position themselves on the high ground. If Lee intended to win, he was going to have to take that high ground—fast.

Always courteous, Lee told Confederate Richard Ewell to take Cemetery Hill, "if possible."[14] Lee meant to take the hill. Ewell heard "if possible" and did not do anything. Meanwhile, the Union Army strengthened its position.

Lee and Longstreet discussed a plan. Delay, said Longstreet. Move the troops around to the east of the fishhook, and we will cut off the Union Army from Washington and leave the capital defenseless. Lee said no. "The enemy is there," said Lee, "and I am going to attack him there." Longstreet argued. Again, Lee said no. "They are in position and I am going to whip them or they are going to whip me."[15]

Lee and his generals talked long into the night. "Gentlemen," said Lee, "we will attack the enemy as early in the morning as possible."[16]

Early on July 2, Lee assumed that the battle would begin at dawn. He waited almost all day. It was late in the afternoon before Longstreet reached his position along the Emmitsburg Road.

The fighting took place in the Peach Orchard, Devil's Den, and Little Round Top. It was bloody. The Confederates managed to take the Peach Orchard, but they did not take Little Round Top. A Maine college teacher named Joshua Chamberlain and a small group of weary soldiers defended it from the Confederates. When the Maine soldiers ran out of ammunition, Chamberlain decided there was only one thing to do: charge with bayonets. The Confederate soldiers ran like "wild cattle."[17]

For Lee, July 2 was a disaster. The Army of Northern Virginia had not taken the high ground. In the afternoon, Stuart and his cavalry arrived—at last. General George Pickett's division had also arrived. Perhaps tomorrow would be a better day.

Early on the morning of July 3, Lee ordered Ewell to attack the enemy on the right while Longstreet delivered the major blow at the center of Cemetery Ridge. Ewell tried, but his attack was repulsed. Longstreet sent General George Pickett.

At noon, an eerie silence fell over the battlefield. The Union Army watched the Confederates push their cannons and artillery into position opposite the center of Cemetery Ridge. A little after 1:00 P.M., Pickett, with his long hair oiled and curled, was ready. "Up, men!" he shouted. "Don't forget today that you are from old Virginia!"[18]

The men in Pickett's charge marched in a straight line, across an open field and uphill toward the Union Army. When one of them was hit, they closed up the line and filled in the gap. Through the woods, across the field, and to the crest of Cemetery Ridge, the Confederates ran forward to their deaths.

One witness wrote,

Men fire into each other's faces, not five feet apart . . . men going down on their hands and knees, spinning round like tops, throwing

out their arms, gulping up blood, falling; legless, armless, headless.
There are ghastly heaps of dead men . . .[19]

It was over in less than an hour. The survivors straggled back, and Lee tried to encourage them. Organize your division of men, he told Pickett. Pickett looked dumbfounded. "General Lee," he replied, "I have no division now."[20]

There was nothing else to do. Lee worked long into the night, organizing the retreat of his army.

At noon on July 4, the rain began to fall in "blinding sheets," as if the heavens were crying.[21] The Confederate ambulance-wagon train stretched seventeen miles and carried some five thousand wounded soldiers. Thousands more remained on the battlefield. Many of the wounded soldiers being transported cried out in pain, begging God to let them die, and many of them did die along the way. At Gettysburg, nearly fifty thousand Union and Confederate soldiers were killed or wounded.

"It's all my fault," Lee told Longstreet. "I thought my men were invincible."[22]

Sometime later, Lee explained that "on the day of battle I lay the fate of my army in the hands of God."[23] Maybe God had spoken on a rainy day at Gettysburg.

The Confederates headed home in the rain.

Chapter 8

APPOMATTOX

What if Stuart had not been missing before the Battle of Gettysburg? What if Ewell had not hesitated when ordered to take the high ground? What if Longstreet had not delayed? Lee did not dwell on the "what ifs." He and his men had done their best.

Besides, there was no time to lay blame. There was no time to mourn or even to sleep. Lee focused his attention on details, on duty. He had to get his army home to Virginia. He would not lose control.

The rain continued. At Williamsport, Maryland, the Potomac River was high and still rising. At Falling Waters, the pontoon bridge had been destroyed. Lee received word that his son Rooney had been captured and taken prisoner. For all Lee knew, the Union Army was close behind, ready to attack. Yet Lee remained calm and cheerful. He focused his attention on details. Lee decided to wait for the river to lower. He would not lose control.

On July 13, nine days after the Battle of Gettysburg, Ewell's men waded across the Potomac River, with the taller men standing in water up to their armpits and passing the shorter men along. A few miles away, horses and wagons rolled across a makeshift pontoon bridge constructed with lumber taken from abandoned homes. When the army was back on Virginia soil, there still was no time to rest. Lee sent the soldiers to the wheat fields, to harvest the crop for food.

While he did not blame his officers or his soldiers for what had gone wrong at Gettysburg, he did find fault with himself. To Jefferson Davis, he said, "I am alone to blame."[1] Lee offered his resignation. Davis refused it.

In the early fall of 1863, Lee focused his attention on the needs of his army. The soldiers needed food, shoes, and socks. Lee needed men. He had lost one third of his troops at Gettysburg. In September, Longstreet left for Georgia, taking more men with him, which left Lee with fewer than fifty thousand soldiers. For the first time, Lee gave orders to shoot deserters. The war escalated on the western front, and Davis wanted Lee to assume command in Tennessee. Lee declined. His duty was to Virginia.

But he was not well. He had a cold, he explained, and rheumatism in his back. For days, he could not ride Traveller; he rode in an ambulance. More than likely, he suffered from angina pectoris, a condition that usually results in a diminished supply of blood to the heart muscle. On the outside, Lee controlled his emotions, but on the inside, his heart was breaking.

There was more fighting. On October 15, at Bristoe Station, Virginia, a small group of Confederate soldiers led by A. P. Hill attacked an entire corps of the Union Army. The Confederates charged down a slope—right into enemy fire. Some fourteen hundred were killed or wounded and four hundred fifty were captured. The disaster seemed senseless. "There was no excuse for it," said one of Lee's aides.[2] Hill acknowledged his mistake. "I am convinced that I made the attack too hastily," he said.[3]

Late in November, while Meade made plans to strike, Lee strengthened his defenses. Meade had more men and guns, but he hesitated. Lee attacked, only to discover that the Union Army had retreated. "I am too old to command this army," Lee sighed, "we should never have permitted those people to get away."[4]

On December 16, Lee went to Richmond to meet with President Davis, and while there, he visited his family. It was not a safe place, and Lee said so, but his wife rented a house there anyway. He had not seen her in seven months. If Lee sought solace and rest, he did not find it with his family. Mrs. Lee was so crippled that she was confined to a wheelchair. Custis was unhappy with his job on President Davis's staff. He wanted a more active part in the war. Rooney was still being held a prisoner of war at Fort Monroe, Virginia. Rooney's wife, Charlotte, was very ill and near death. All of them longed for Arlington House, now "officially" taken over by the United States government.

Lee did not even stay for Christmas. On December 21, he returned to the Army of Northern Virginia, where he spent the holiday in a tent. His staff was not surprised. Duty before "personal desire," as one of his staff explained.[5]

In the winter of 1864, Lee focused his attention on details—socks. His wife, his daughters, and their friends knitted some four hundred pairs of socks for Lee's soldiers. In one letter after another, Lee told Mary that the socks had arrived, but that she had not counted them correctly. Counting socks was an odd thing for a general to do. Maybe the war was getting to Lee.

Lee and his men waited for the spring campaign to begin. Winter weather made traveling difficult. Dirt roads often turned into thick mud. While they waited, Lee organized his army. The Confederate government extended the age limits of the draft—seventeen-year-old boys and fifty-year-old men were declared fit to fight. Longstreet and his men were heading back to Virginia. Lee's son Rooney was free, having been exchanged as a prisoner of war. At best, Lee would have a force of roughly sixty thousand men.

The Union Army had more than a hundred thousand soldiers, and once again, the Union Army had a new commanding general. Meade kept his title as the General of the Army of the Potomac, but Ulysses S. Grant took charge. He was named the Commanding General of all the Union Armies.

The Wilderness, 1864

On May 4, 1864, the Union Army crossed the Rapidan River at two places, right into Lee's hands. The Union soldiers found themselves in the Wilderness, just where they had been whipped a year ago. Around the Union campfires that evening, soldiers listened to the sad song of the whippoorwill. They looked at the half-buried skeletons of the Union soldiers who had died there and were rotting there. Only the "devil and old man Lee" would pick such a place for a fight.[6]

The battle started on the morning of May 5. One word best described fighting in the Wilderness, and that was panic. The woods were so thick and full of briars that the men lost all sense of direction. They could not see. "A battle of invisibles with invisibles," declared one veteran. It wasn't fighting, said another, but "bushwhacking."[7]

Longstreet was late, again. Lee looked for him in the afternoon, in the evening hours, at midnight. Early on the morning of May 6, the Union Army attacked, and the exhausted Confederates ran scared. They ran "like a flock of geese," said Lee.[8] It looked like it was over.

When Longstreet finally arrived with his Texas brigade leading the way, Lee was beside himself. He charged to the front with the Texans, waving his hat and shouting, "Hurrah for Texas!"[9] Frantic, the men tried to get Lee to go to the rear of the action, but he paid no attention until a sergeant grabbed Traveller by the reins. At that, Lee calmed down and moved to a safer position.

Around 10:00 A.M.., an uneasy silence settled over the Wilderness, the sort of silence that "precedes the tornado."[10] At 11:00 A.M., the woods exploded with the sounds of the Rebel yell. Grant had both flanks unguarded and a long gap in the center. For the next seven hours, the Confederates made him pay for these mistakes.

"Rebel Yell"

The rebel yell was a high-pitched scream that scared more than one Yankee soldier. Today, however, the yell has been completely lost. No one really knows how it sounded. Many years after the war, one old Confederate soldier was asked to do the rebel yell at a picnic. He declined. He claimed that the yell had to be "made in a dead run in full charge against the enemy," and it certainly could not be made "with a stomach full of food and a mouth full of false teeth."[11]

Longstreet fought long and hard, and toward the end of the afternoon, he was accidentally shot by his own men. It was less than a mile from where Stonewall's men had shot him a year ago. Blood gurgled from Longstreet's throat as he was carried from the field, but he did not die.[12]

That night, a brisk wind carried sparks from campfires into dead pine trees, and the trees blazed into twenty-foot-tall torches. Cartridge boxes exploded. Bits of charges in soldiers' pockets exploded. The wounded screamed. For all they knew, they were in hell.[13]

Lee had whipped Grant. Before, when Lee had beaten other Union generals, they had retreated, but Grant was different. "There will be no turning back," he said.[14]

Instead, Grant moved. On May 8, his army headed southeast some twelve miles away to a place called Spotsylvania Court House in Virginia. Lee figured out Grant's plans and beat him there. By May 9, Lee's men had cut down trees, dug a trench, and established a defensive line. The north end of the line stuck out, and the soldiers called it the Mule Shoe. Late in the afternoon on May 10, Grant's men attacked the Mule Shoe, but they were quickly repulsed. On May 11, Grant did not attack, and Lee made a serious mistake. He decided that Grant was on the move again, and as a result, he ordered his men to leave their positions and prepare to march.

But Grant was not going anywhere. Early on May 12, he struck the Mule Shoe again. Although some Confederates were still there, they were no match for the Union forces. In less than half an hour, twenty-five hundred of them were either shot or captured. Lee saw his men running away. Again, Lee charged the enemy before an officer led him to a safer spot. "These men," said the officer, "have never failed you. They never will."[15]

The Union Army came fast and furious. Twenty thousand Union soldiers were jammed together so tightly that they could not even raise their arms. The Confederates shot at them. A shell burst near Traveller, and if he had not reared, Lee would have been hit.

The Mule Shoe took on another name—the Bloody Angle. Worse than anything in the Wilderness, the Bloody Angle was "concentrated terror."[16] It was raining, and the ground became a bloody, muddy slime. To shoot, soldiers stood on top of dead men, and some of the piles were twenty men deep. There was so much gunfire that an oak tree, twenty-two inches in diameter, was smashed into kindling wood. The bloody nightmare continued for sixteen unrelenting hours.

In the midst of this horror, Lee received word that Stuart was dying, shot by Union cavalry at Yellow Tavern, Virginia, north of Richmond.

The next morning, while it continued to rain, the exhausted soldiers stretched out in the mud and slept. In eight days, Lee lost some eighteen thousand men, one third of his army. Grant lost some thirty-six thousand men.[17] By the body count, Lee had won, but Grant would not retreat.

On May 20, Grant moved southeast again, to Cold Harbor, Virginia, which was an old British name meaning a place to rest and to get cold food. Lee's army was ready.

The Confederates dug in and fortified a seven-mile line of defense. Several times Grant pushed, but he could not break the Confederate line. On July 2, Grant ordered the Union Army to prepare for a major attack. After supper, Union soldiers sewed their names on their jackets, so that their dead bodies could be identified. (Dog tags had not yet been invented.) One soldier wrote in his diary. "June 3. Cold Harbor. I was killed."[18] He was.

At dawn on June 3, 1864, thousands of Union soldiers attacked the Confederates, roaring, "Huzzah, Huzzah!"[19] In eight minutes, Grant lost seven thousand men. They did not break Lee's line.

Grant would not admit that he had lost. Ordinarily, a defeated general sent a flag of truce to the winner, asking to be allowed to collect his wounded and dead soldiers from the battlefield. But Grant was stubborn. The wounded cried. The bodies of the dead swelled up and rotted. "Grant intends to stink Lee out of his position," wrote a Confederate.[20] On June 7, four days after the battle, Grant called for a flag of truce. Only two men on the battlefield were still alive.

Grant did not retreat. He moved southeast, again, crossing the James River. Lee stayed where he was, uncertain as to Grant's plan of action. At last, Lee had met his match as a general.

No Union General Could Outwit Lee

The Union Army was superior to the Confederate Army in many ways except they did not have a general who could outwit Robert E. Lee. In late 1863, after Meade retreated rather than attacking Lee's smaller army, President Lincoln said that Meade reminded him of "an old woman trying to shoo her geese across a creek."[21]

Grant managed to beat Lee, but many believe that he did it not by outwitting Lee, but by sacrificing his men. During six weeks of fighting in the spring and early summer of 1864, some one hundred thousand Union soldiers were killed or wounded. "He is a butcher," said Mary Todd Lincoln of Grant, "and is not fit to be at the head of an army."[22]

But it was not long before Lee figured out Grant's plans. The Union Army was heading toward Petersburg, the back door to Richmond. This was a smart move for two reasons. First, if Grant took Petersburg, he could choke the Confederate capital of Richmond, isolating it from the rest of the Confederacy. Second, if Lee's soldiers dug in and defended Petersburg, they would be prevented from moving about freely and living off the land, which meant that they would slowly starve. "This army can not stand a siege," Lee said.[23] The siege of Petersburg was about to begin.

The Confederate Army started digging. They stretched their line of defense some thirty miles around Petersburg and dug six-foot-deep ditches. They cut down trees, laid them out, and sharpened their branches. Then, they dug caves and lived underground. Lee's army did not intend to give up Petersburg.

Grant did not intend to retreat. That summer, Union soldiers dug a 511-foot-long underground tunnel that ended inside the Confederate line. On July 23, 1864, the Union Army exploded an underground bomb—ripping out a huge, gaping crater. Dirt and men flew skyward. In the confusion, thousands of Union soldiers became trapped in the hole, and when the Confederates saw that some of these men were African-American soldiers, they went berserk.[24] Confederate soldiers stood on the rim of the crater and fired away at the Northern troops, killing and wounding four thousand men before the battle was over.

Summer passed. Fall passed. Winter came. The Army of Northern Virginia began to starve. The soldiers' daily ration consisted of a small handful of cornmeal and about an ounce of Nassau bacon that the Confederates nicknamed Nausea bacon—it stretched when chewed. One soldier remarked, "I thanked God I had a backbone for my stomach to lean up against."[25] They still had a sense of humor, but it was not enough. It was just a matter of time.

The Final Days

On January 31, 1865, the Confederate Congress made Lee the general in chief of all the Confederate Armies. The Civil War was not only fought in the East. In the West, fighting occurred in Tennessee and along the Mississippi River. In the South, Union General William Tecumseh Sherman was leading a devastating march from Atlanta to the sea and was now making his way north to Virginia. Although Lee accepted the title, he continued to focus his attention on the Army of Northern Virginia. Even with the promotion, Lee could not get food for his army.

On February 3, 1865, three Confederate officials secretly met with President Lincoln aboard the presidential steamer the *River Queen*. Both sides discussed a way to end the war. President Lincoln did not intend to punish the South. His demands were simple—the Southern states must agree to stop the resistance and to free the slaves. The Confederates refused, calling it an "unconditional surrender."[26]

By March 1865, thousands of soldiers had deserted the Army of Northern Virginia. The Confederate government was so desperate for soldiers that it passed a law allowing slaves to fight for the Southern cause. Not surprisingly, nothing much came of this law.

Early on the morning of March 25, the Army of Northern Virginia attacked the Union forces at Fort Stedman near Petersburg. They took the fort, but could not hold it, having lost four thousand men. Lee's army slipped away. It was their last attack.

On April 2, 1865, Grant's army broke Lee's line. The Confederates retreated from Petersburg, heading north to the Appomattox River. The men marched westward toward Amelia Court House, where Lee said that food and supplies would be waiting. For some reason, when they arrived, there was no food. Lee ordered an all night march on April 5 toward Farmville, toward food. Instead, they found themselves attacked by Union cavalry. Almost half of the Confederates panicked and ran. Lee ordered the remaining men to press on toward Appomattox Court House, still hoping to find food. They were repulsed by Union forces. The end was near.

"Then there is nothing left me but to go and see General Grant," said Lee, "and I would rather die a thousand deaths."[27]

On April 9, 1865, Palm Sunday, Confederate General Robert E. Lee met with Union General Ulysses S. Grant at Wilmer

McLean's house in Appomattox Court House, Virginia. Lee arrived first and waited in the parlor. He wore his best uniform, a red silk sash, and his sword.

General Grant arrived spattered with mud and with his coat unbuttoned. The two men shook hands. For a few minutes, Grant chatted about their time in the Mexican War. Lee turned the conversation to the real reason they were there. He asked about the terms of the surrender. Grant was generous.

The War Began in His Backyard
and Ended in His Parlor

At the beginning of the war, Wilmer McLean had owned a farm near Bull Run in Virginia, but after the second battle there, he moved his family to Appomattox Court House, Virginia, where he hoped they would be safer. At the end of the war, the parlor of McLean's farmhouse was chosen as the best place for Grant and Lee to meet. After the two generals left, scavengers, in hopes of grabbing historical relics, carted off many of McLean's possessions.

The terms were these: After the men surrendered, they would be released instead of imprisoned. As long as they promised not to bear arms against the United States, they were free to go home, free to plant a spring crop. Men could keep their side arms. They could keep their horses and mules.

Grant also sent twenty-five thousand rations to feed Lee's army.

Papers were signed and sealed. The two generals shook hands. Outside, Lee mounted Traveller. Grant removed his hat in salute, and his officers followed his example. Lee returned the salute and left.

There was silence.

Back with his own army, his men crowded around him. "General, are we surrendered?" they asked.[28]

Tears streamed down Lee's face. He had lost his self-control. "I have done the best I could for you," he said, stumbling over his words. Then, in a whisper, Lee said, "Goodbye."[29]

Chapter 9

AFTER THE WAR

On the evening of April 15, 1865—the day that President Lincoln was assassinated by John Wilkes Booth—Lee arrived on the outskirts of Richmond. It was raining. Two weeks earlier, fire had destroyed much of the city. Banks were closed. Store shelves were bare. Surely Lee saw the destruction. Surely Lee knew that he shared some of the blame for thousands of sorrows. But he said nothing.

At 707 East Franklin Street, he dismounted Traveller and went inside to his family. He was very tired. For the next few weeks, he slept and rested. When awake, he sat in silence.

People wanted to see Lee, to speak with him. Thomas Cook, a reporter for the *New York Herald*, came to interview him. Mathew Brady, the famous Civil War photographer, came to take his picture. Reluctantly, Lee stood on the back porch. The camera captured his suntanned cheeks, his pale forehead, his balding scalp, his black eyes, and his defiant stance. Even a Confederate soldier came to the house, wanting to meet the general before he started his long walk home to Texas. But when the Texan saw Lee, he burst into tears and turned away. Lee said nothing.[1]

The news of Appomattox spread. One by one, the remaining Confederate Armies surrendered until finally, on May 26, 1865, the Civil War was finally over. Some two hundred fifty thousand Confederate soldiers were dead, and thousands more were permanently injured. Millions of newly freed African Americans were left to fend for themselves, homeless and uneducated. Farms, banks, and businesses were destroyed. A hard-biting bitterness spread over the land, and even today, one can sometimes still taste it. The future looked bleak. In June 1865, Lee was formally charged with treason, for making war against the United States.

Lee had understood that he and his men had been given amnesty, protection from such charges. He turned to Grant for help, and Grant saw to it that the charges against Lee were dropped. Lee asked for a pardon from President Andrew Johnson. The pardon did not come easily. In fact, Lee's full citizenship was not restored until 1975, more than a hundred years after his death.

Lee's Lost Pardon

On October 2, 1865, Robert E. Lee signed a written pledge of allegiance to the United States, asking that his civil rights be restored. In Washington, D.C., the pardon went to the desk of the secretary of state, William H. Seward, where it was misplaced and forgotten—for over a hundred years. When Lee did not receive a reply, he assumed that his request had been denied. In the summer of 1975, after his pardon was found in some papers in the National Archives, the United States Congress passed a bill signed by President Gerald R. Ford that restored citizenship to Lee.[2]

In 1865, hot-headed Southerners thought that Lee's request for pardon showed that he was admitting defeat. But Lee was beyond anger. Lee sought peace, and he urged other ex-Confederates to do the same.

Sometimes, however, he said harsh things about African Americans. "[W]herever you find the negro," Lee told a cousin, "everything is going down around him."[3] Virginia would be better off without them, he said. Yet his actions did not match his words. At Richmond's St. Paul's Church that summer, when an African American stepped forward to take communion, the white congregation froze—except for Lee. Alone, he went to the altar and knelt beside the man.

The summer of 1865 slipped away. Lee, a man who believed in doing his duty, had nothing to do.

Washington College

Lee needed a job, a way to support his family. An insurance company offered him ten thousand dollars for the use of his name. Lee rejected the offer. In August 1865, an official from Washington College, a poor, struggling school for young men in Lexington, Virginia, asked Lee to become the school's president for a yearly salary of fifteen hundred dollars. Lee accepted.

Lee declined the college's plan for a showy inauguration. Instead, on the morning of October 2, 1865, after a short ceremony in the physics classroom, Lee went to his office to work.

As always, he focused his attention on details. First, he tackled the mail—piled high in a laundry basket—and answered it all himself. He kept track of each student's progress. When one boy failed to study, Lee did not chastise him for his laziness. Instead, he wrote to his parent, "He . . . seems very careful not to injure the health of his father's son."[4] Lee organized and directed the repair of the buildings and grounds. He worked on the curriculum, the plan of courses offered by the college.

Under Lee's leadership, Washington College combined classical courses with practical ones. The college gave the students more choices by offering courses in agriculture, business, engineering, Spanish, French, and German. They held one of the first summer schools in the country. Lee dreamed of building an observatory, so that students could study the stars.

Lee—who had spent a lifetime following orders and regulations—started doing away with certain rules. Students were no longer required to attend morning chapel, but to set an example, Lee attended every morning. As he explained, "We have but one rule here, and it is that every student must be a gentleman."[5]

Lee had more than his share of opportunities that required him to be a gentleman. Before his death, President Lincoln had seen Reconstruction as a time of healing, but the radical Republicans in the United States Congress saw it as a way of punishing the South. In February 1866, Lee was summoned to a congressional hearing in Washington, D.C., where he was interrogated about the loyalty of Virginians to the United States. After two hours of calmly answering questions, Lee was released. In November 1867, Lee was summoned to a federal jury investigating whether or not former Confederate President Jefferson Davis should be tried for treason. Eventually, the case was dropped. In Lexington, during the winter of 1868, several Washington College students got mixed up in a fight with a young African American. They tied a rope around his neck, then dragged him through the town. Lee expelled the students. Still, the *New York Independent Newspaper* blamed Lee for the actions of the hot-headed young men and declared that Lee was not fit to lead students.[6]

"I am considered now such a monster," Lee wrote.[7] To a student, Lee explained the importance of controlling one's thoughts. "If it had not been for this power," he explained, "I do not see how I could have stood what I had to go through with."[8]

By focusing his attention on details, Lee's days were pleasant enough. He expected his wife and daughters to be at the breakfast table by 7:00 A.M., where they often found a rose waiting for each of them. He worked at the office until two o'clock, when he came home for dinner. Afterward, he took a brief nap, while sitting and having his hands rubbed by one of his daughters. Lee edited his father's Revolutionary War memoirs, publishing them in 1868, but he never got around to describing his own years at war. He enjoyed long rides on Traveller, friendships with children, and cheerful light-hearted conversations with women.

By focusing his attention on his students, Lee had a reason for living. He turned down a job with a big salary. "I have led the young men of the South in battle . . . [and] seen many of them die, . . ." he wrote, "I shall devote my remaining energies to training young men."[9]

While he never admitted that he had been wrong in fighting for the South, his words and actions began to reflect his true feelings. "The great mistake of my life," he said, "was taking a military education."[10] To one of his former officers, Lee wrote, "I have wasted the best years of my existence."[11]

When the students and teachers of Washington College and Virginia Military Institute marched in parade to the beat of a drum, Lee—a man who had always followed regulations— deliberately marched out of step.

In the spring of 1870, sixty-three-year-old Lee could barely walk the short distance from his house to his office, and he began to talk of retiring. Lee's doctors persuaded him to take a trip South, believing warmer weather would make him feel better.

Arlington National Cemetery

In 1864, United States Quartermaster Montgomery Meigs was ordered to find a new site for a Union cemetery. A Georgian by birth, Meigs had remained loyal to the Union. Meigs, who had served under Lee at St. Louis, Missouri, chose to bury the dead at Arlington House, thereby ensuring that the house would never again be a home. When Meigs's son was killed by Confederate cavalry, he buried him on the grounds of the Lee mansion.

Lee and his daughter Mildred set off on what became Lee's farewell tour.

They went by train to Richmond, Virginia; to Raleigh, North Carolina; and to Savannah, Georgia. They visited the graves of his daughter Annie and his father, Light-Horse Harry Lee. Along the way, people lined up beside the train tracks, hoping for a chance to see Lee. There was something about him that people respected. One of his young female cousins exclaimed, "We had heard of God, but here was General Lee."[12]

The trip did not improve Lee's health. No doubt, he was suffering from hardening of the arteries, a disease that had not yet been identified.

In July 1870, Lee tried one more time to recover Arlington House from the United States government, but it was hopeless. Since 1864, the property had been used as a military cemetery, with some sixteen thousand Union soldiers already buried on the lawns. "[P]lanted," as Mrs. Lee said, "up to the very door."[13] Eventually, the government reimbursed their son Custis for the family home, which became better known as the Arlington National Cemetery.

The afternoon of September 28, 1870, was chilly and rainy, and Lee took a nap sitting up. His daughter Agnes rubbed his hands. On the piano, Mildred first played a piece from "Songs Without Words," then "The Funeral March," both by Mendelssohn. Lee had a meeting at Grace Church. "I wish I did not have to go and listen to all that powwow," he said.[14]

But at the church, Lee acted cheerful. The meeting lasted for hours. They were short fifty-five dollars for the minister's salary. At last Lee said, "I will give that sum."[15]

He walked home in the rain, and when he arrived, Mary teased him for being late for supper—Lee was always on time. He stood at his place at the table as if to say grace. He tried to speak, but there was silence. More than likely, Lee had suffered a stroke.

For two weeks, he lingered near death. It rained so hard that the streets flooded. Mary and his daughters sat beside him. They wanted him to say something, anything. Once, according to his wife, Lee said, "Tell [General] Hill he must come up! Strike the tent!"[16] But Mildred remembered it differently. "His lips never uttered a sound," she wrote. "The silence was awful."[17]

On October 12, 1870, Lee died. Three days later, in the college chapel, the mourners sang Lee's favorite hymn, "How Firm a Foundation," but there was no sermon, as Lee had requested. There would be no final words to explain Robert E. Lee.

It was over.

Chapter 10

"I Have Already Led Enough Forlorn Hopes"

R obert E. Lee is often remembered as a Southern hero of the Civil War. He was an excellent general. Cunning and aggressive, he could beat superior armies. But there was more to Lee than that.

He devoted the last years of his life to the education of young men. "It seems to me that I have already led enough forlorn hopes," he explained.[1] After his death, Washington College became Washington and Lee University, renamed in his honor. Today, it is one of the best schools in the country. There is even an observatory there so that students can study the stars. Washington and Lee University is his finest legacy.

To be sure, Lee was good at war. But perhaps the people who admire Lee for this reason miss the larger lesson of his life. Lee experienced great success, and he endured devastating failure. When confronted with loss, he did not become bitter or hateful; he just kept on trying. He did his best. In the end, it was not his ability on the battlefield but his devotion to others that redeemed him. His personal sense of duty—always a strength and a weakness—helped shape his character, helped shape history, and earned him a place as an American hero.

CHRONOLOGY

1807—Born at Stratford Hall, Virginia, on January 19.

1818—Father Henry "Light-Horse Harry" dies on March 25, and is buried in Georgia.

1825—Arrives at West Point Military Academy in June.

1829—Graduates second in his class at West Point. Mother Ann Hill Carter dies on July 26; Reports for duty at Cockspur Island, Georgia, in November.

1831—Reports for duty at Fort Monroe, Virginia, in June; Marries Mary Ann Randolph Custis on June 30.

1832—Son George Washington Custis is born.

1835—Daughter Mary Custis is born.

1837—Son William Henry Fitzhugh (Rooney) is born; Reports for duty in St. Louis, Missouri, in August.

1839—Daughter Anne is born.

1840—Reports for duty at Fort Hamilton in Brooklyn, New York, and serves as engineer.

1841—Daughter Agnes is born.

1843—Son Robert Edward, Jr. (Rob) is born.

1846—Daughter Mildred is born.

1846—Serves as advisor to General Winfield Scott in Mexico during the war with Mexico.

1852—Serves as superintendent of West Point Military Academy.

1856—Reports for duty in Texas as second in command of the 2nd Cavalry.

1859—Returns home to Virginia to manage the Custis estates; Serves as commanding officer at Harpers Ferry on October 17, 1859.

1860—Returns to San Antonio to command the United States Military Department in Texas in February.

1861—Declines assignment as commander of the United States Army and resigns on April 20; Accepts command of military and naval forces of Virginia on April 22; Acquires his horse Traveller.

1862—Accepts position as commanding general of the Army of Northern Virginia on June 1; Directs the battles of: Seven Days, Virginia on June 25–July 1; Second Battle of Bull Run on August 27–30; Antietam, Maryland on September 17; and Fredericksburg, Virginia on December 13; Daughter Annie dies.

1863—Directs the battles at: Chancellorsville, Virginia on May 1–4; Gettysburg, Pennsylvania on July 1–3.

1864—Directs the battles in Virginia at: the Wilderness, May 5–6; Spotsylvania Court House on May 8–19; Cold Harbor on June 1–3; Begins the siege of Petersburg on June 20.

1865—Continues the siege of Petersburg through April. Surrenders to United States General Ulysses S. Grant on April 9; Accepts position as president of Washington College on October 2.

1866—Continues to serve as president of Washington College; Dies on October 12, 1870.

Chapter Notes

Chapter 1

1. Carl Coke Rister, *Robert E. Lee in Texas* (Norman, Okla.: University of Oklahoma Press, 1946), pp. 150–151.

2. John Salmon Ford, *Rip Ford's Texas*, ed. Stephen B. Oates (Austin: University of Texas Press, 1987), p. 305.

3. Rister, p. 167.

4. Ibid., p. 150.

5. Emory M. Thomas, *Robert E. Lee, A Biography* (New York: Norton, 1995), p. 171.

6. Richard Harwell, *Lee: An Abridgment in One Volume of the Four-Volume R. E. Lee by Douglas Southall Freeman* (New York: Collier, 1993), p. 104.

7. Thomas, pp. 184–185.

8. Marquis James, *The Raven, A Biography of Sam Houston* (Austin: University of Texas Press, 1988), p. 408.

9. Rister, p. 165.

10. Ford, pp. 305–306; Thomas, pp. 167, 170, 185.

11. Rister, p. 126.

12. Thomas, p. 186.

13. Harwell, p. 106.

14. Ibid.

15. Rister, p. 157.

16. Ibid.

17. Ibid., p. 159.

18. Thomas, p. 187.

19. Freeman, p. 109.

20. Ibid., p. 392.

Chapter 2

1. Emory M. Thomas, *Robert E. Lee, A Biography* (New York: Norton, 1995), p. 24.

2. Ibid., p. 25.

3. Ibid., p. 24.

4. Ibid., pp. 25–26.

5. Douglas Southall Freeman, *R. E. Lee, A Biography* (New York: Scribners, 1935), vol. 1, p. 12.

6. Henry Lee, *Memoirs of the War Southern Department of the United States*, ed. *Robert E. Lee* (New York: University Publishing, 1870), p. 65; A letter from General Henry Lee to C. C. Lee, Nassau, February 9, 1817.

7. A. L. Long, *Memoirs of Robert E. Lee: His Military and Personal History* (Secaucus, N.J.: Blue and Grey Press, 1983), p. 21.

8. Richard Harwell, *Lee: An Abridgment in One Volume of the Four-Volume R. E. Lee by Douglas Southall Freeman* (New York: Collier, 1993), p. 10.

9. Thomas, p. 31.

10. Freeman, p. 20.

11. Paul C. Nagel, *The Lees of Virginia: Seven Generations of an American Family* (New York: Oxford, 1990), p. 232.

12. Freeman, pp. 18–19.

13. J. William Jones, *Personal Reminiscences, Anecdotes, and Letters of Gen. Robert E. Lee* (New York: Appleton, 1875), p. 363.

14. Thomas, p. 38.

15. Nagel, p. 198.

16. Jones, p. 362.

17. Ibid., p. 366.

Chapter 3

1. A. L. Long, *Memoirs of Robert E. Lee: His Military and Personal History* (Secaucus, N.J.: Blue and Grey Press, 1983), p. 30.

2. Richard Harwell, *Lee: An Abridgment in One Volume of the Four-Volume R. E. Lee by Douglas Southall Freeman* (New York: Collier, 1993), p. 12.

3. Calhoun believed in states' rights, and to some extent, his theories helped fuel the Civil War.

4. Douglas Southall Freeman, *R. E. Lee, A Biography* (New York: Scribners, 1935), vol. 1, p. 39.

5. Ibid., p. 40.

6. Ibid., p. 41.

7. Ibid., p. 44.

8. Ibid., p. 46.

9. Ibid., p. 47.

10. Emory M. Thomas, *Robert E. Lee, A Biography* (New York: Norton, 1995), pp. 48–49.

11. Ibid., p. 49.

12. Ibid., p. 50.

13. Freeman, p. 17.

14. Thomas, p. 54.

15. Freeman, p. 68.

16. Long, p. 30.

Chapter 4

1. A. L. Long, *Memoirs of Robert E. Lee: His Military and Personal History* (Secaucus, N.J.: Blue and Grey Press, 1983), p. 26.

2. Emory M. Thomas, *Robert E. Lee, A Biography* (New York: Norton, 1995), pp. 45, 191, 367.

3. Robert E. Lee brought one of the family's elderly slaves with him. Too old to work, Nat died in Georgia the next year.

4. Richard Harwell, *Lee: An Abridgment in One Volume of the Four-Volume R. E. Lee by Douglas Southall Freeman* (New York: Collier, 1993), p. 27.

5. Thomas, pp. 65, 93.

6. Douglas Southall Freeman, *R. E. Lee, A Biography* (New York: Scribners, 1935), vol. 1, p. 93.

7. Ibid., p. 46.

8. Thomas, pp. 84, 83.

9. Ibid., p. 65.

10. Ibid., p. 64.

11. Freeman, p. 110.

12. Thomas, pp. 70–71.

13. Ibid., p. 66.

14. Ibid., p. 71.

15. Ibid., p. 73.

16. Ibid., p. 82.

17. Long, p. 44.

18. Thomas, pp. 103–105.

19. Ibid., p. 72.

20. Ibid., p. 106.

21. Ibid., p. 107.

Chapter 5

1. A. L. Long, *Memoirs of Robert E. Lee: His Military and Personal History* (Secaucus, N.J.: Blue and Grey Press, 1983), p. 52.

2. Ibid., p. 57.

3. Ibid., p. 140.

4. Ibid., p. 61.

5. Emory M. Thomas, *Robert E. Lee, A Biography* (New York: Norton, 1995), p. 127.

6. Ibid., p. 119.

7. Robert E. Lee, *Recollections and Letters of General Robert E. Lee by His Son Captain Robert E. Lee* (Garden City, N.Y.: Garden City Publishing, 1924), p. 4.

8. Ibid., pp. 6, 9–10.

9. Thomas, p. 152.

10. Ibid.

11. Ibid., p. 155.

12. Douglas Southall Freeman, *R. E. Lee, A Biography* (New York: Scribners, 1935), vol. 1, p. 364.

13. Ibid., pp. 368–369.

14. Paul C. Nagel, *The Lees of Virginia: Seven Generations of an American Family* (New York: Oxford, 1990), p. 253.

15. Thomas, p. 390.

16. Freeman, p. 372.

17. Ibid., p. 392.

Chapter 6

1. Robert E. Lee, *Recollections and Letters of General Robert E. Lee by His Son Captain Robert E. Lee* (Garden City, N.Y.: Garden City Publishing, 1924), p. 26.

2. Douglas Southall Freeman, *Lee of Virginia* (New York: Scribners, 1958), pp. 58–59.

3. Emory M. Thomas, *Robert E. Lee, A Biography* (New York: Norton, 1995), p. 192. This is how Walter Taylor, who served on Lee's staff, remembered Lee on that day.

4. Richard Harwell, *Lee: An Abridgment in One Volume of the Four-Volume R. E. Lee by Douglas Southall Freeman* (New York: Collier, 1993), pp. 126–127.

5. Ibid.

6. Thomas, p. 210.

7. A. L. Long, *Memoirs of Robert E. Lee: His Military and Personal History* (Secaucus, N.J.: Blue and Grey Press, 1983), pp. 131–133.

8. Clifford Dowdey, ed., *The Wartime Papers of R. E. Lee* (New York: Little, Brown, & Co., 1961), p. 150. Lee's letter to General John Pemberton is dated April 20, 1862.

9. Ibid.

10. Thomas, p. 230.

11. Ibid., p. 223.

12. Ibid., p. 225.

13. Shelby Foote, *The Civil War, A Narrative: Fort Sumter to Perryville* (New York: Random House, 1958), vol. 1, p. 513.

14. Thomas, p. 290.

15. C. Vann Woodward, ed., *Mary Chestnut's Civil War* (New Haven, Conn.: Yale University Press, 1981), p. 116.

16. Dowdey, p. 293. Lee's letter to Jefferson Davis is dated September 2, 1862.

17. Nancy Scott Anderson and Dwight Anderson, *The Generals: Ulysses S. Grant and Robert E. Lee* (New York: Knopf, 1987), p. 264.

18. Foote, p. 668.

19. Lee, Recollections, p. 78.

20. James Longstreet, "The Battle of Fredericksburg," in *Battles and Leaders of the Civil War* (Secaucus, N.J.: Castle, n.d.), vol. 3, p. 70.

21. Walter H. Taylor, *Four Years with General Lee* (Bloomington: Indiana University Press, 1962), p. 76.

22. Freeman, *Lee of Virginia*, p. 103.

Chapter 7

1. Shelby Foote, *The Civil War, A Narrative: Fredericksburg to Meridian* (New York: Random House, 1963), vol. 2, p. 237.

2. Ibid., p. 43.

3. Ibid., p. 249.

4. Emory M. Thomas, *Robert E. Lee, A Biography* (New York: Norton, 1995), p. 277.

5. Foote, p. 262.

6. Ibid., p. 311.

7. Ibid., p. 319.

8. Ibid., p. 446.

9. Glenn Tucker, *High Tide at Gettysburg* (Gettysburg: Stan Clark Military Books, 1995), p. 42.

10. Foote, p. 444.

11. Nancy Scott Anderson and Dwight Anderson, *The Generals: Ulysses S. Grant and Robert E. Lee* (New York: Knopf, 1987), p. 324.

12. Foote, p. 468.

13. Thomas, p. 295.

14. *The American Heritage Picture History of the Civil War* (New York: American Heritage, 1960), p. 332.

15. Tucker, p. 187.

16. Clifford Dowdey, *Lee* (Boston: Little, Brown, & Company, 1965), p. 372.

17. Foote, p. 505.

18. Richard Harwell, *Lee, An Abridgment in One Volume of the Four-Volume R. E. Lee by Douglas Southall Freeman* (New York: Collier, 1993), p. 338.

19. E. B. Long, *The Civil War Day by Day: An Almanac 1861–1865, with Barbara Long* (Garden City, N.Y.: Doubleday, 1971), p. 1863.

20. Harwell, p. 340.

21. John D. Imboden, "*The Confederate Retreat from Gettysburg,*" in *Battles and Leaders of the Civil War* (Secaucus, N.J.: Castle, n.d.), vol. 3, p. 423.

22. Anderson, p. 350.

23. Foote, p. 538.

Chapter 8

1. Clifford Dowdey, *The Wartime Papers of Robert E. Lee* (New York: Da Capo Press, 1961), p. 565.

2. Shelby Foote, *The Civil War, A Narrative: Fredericksburg to Meridian* (New York: Random House, 1963), vol. 2, p. 793.

3. Ibid.

4. Charles S. Venable, "*General Lee in the Wilderness Campaign,*" in *Battles and Leaders of the Civil War* (Secaucus, N.J.: Castle, n.d.), vol. 4, p. 240.

5. Foote, vol. 2, p. 887.

6. Shelby Foote, *The Civil War, A Narrative: Red River to Appomattox* (New York: Random House, 1974), vol. 3, p. 150.

7. Ibid., p. 155.

8. Ibid., p. 169.

9. Ibid.

10. Ibid., p. 171.

11. Ibid., p. 1046.

12. Emory M. Thomas, *Robert E. Lee, A Biography* (New York: Norton, 1995), p. 325.

13. Foote, vol. 3, p. 183.

14. Ibid., p. 186.

15. Ibid., p. 218.

16. Ibid., p. 221.

17. Ibid., p. 241.

18. Ibid., p. 290.

19. Ibid.

20. Ibid., p. 295.

21. Foote, vol. 2, p. 799.

22. David Herbert Donald, *Lincoln* (New York: Simon & Schuster, 1995) p. 513.

23. Foote, vol. 3, p. 317.

24. Thomas, p. 342.

25. Foote, vol. 3, p. 629.

26. Donald, p. 558.

27. Thomas, p. 362.

28. Foote, vol. 3, p. 951.

29. Ibid.

Chapter 9

1. Clifford Dowdey, *Lee* (Boston: Little Brown, 1965), p. 636.

2. Emory M. Thomas, *Robert E. Lee, A Biography* (New York: Norton, 1995), p. 381.

3. Ibid., p. 372.

4. Ibid., p. 398.

5. Ibid., p. 397.

6. Ibid., p. 389.

7. Ibid., p. 381.

8. Thomas L. Connelly, *The Marble Man, Robert E. Lee and His Image in American Society* (Baton Rouge: Louisiana State Press), p. 189.

9. Charles Bracelen Flood, *Lee, The Last Years* (Boston: Houghton Mifflin, 1981), p. 175.

10. Ibid., p. 156.

11. Ibid., p. 175.

12. Ibid., p. 246.

13. Connelly, p. 34.

14. Flood, p. 256.

15. Ibid.

16. Ibid., p. 261.

17. Ibid., p. 259.

Chapter 10

1. Robert W. Winston, *Robert E. Lee* (New York: Morrow, 1934), p. 407.

Glossary

abolitionist—A person who believes in doing away with slavery.

blue norther—A strong, icy, arctic wind that blows in suddenly across the Texas plains. Within minutes, temperatures can drop fifty degrees.

"Butternut"—Confederate soldiers were sometimes called Butternuts because their cotton uniforms turned into a yellow-brown color, bleached out by the sun.

cavalry—An army on horseback. By riding fast and covering large territories, the cavalry provided vital information about the enemy.

Confederate—A term used to identify those who fought for the Confederacy. Eleven states withdrew from the United States of America. The Confederate States of America included: Alabama, Arkansas, Florida, Georgia, Louisiana, Mississippi, North Carolina, South Carolina, Tennessee, Texas, and Virginia.

engineer—A person who uses mathematics and science to build something.

flank—A term to describe the far right or far left side of a military formation.

observatory—A building that has a telescope and other equipment to study the stars.

"Rebel"—A nickname for a Confederate.

reconnaissance—A military term which means to survey the land in order to discover the strength and position of the enemy.

Reconstruction—Lasting from 1865 to 1877, it was a controversial attempt to rebuild the South after the Civil War. Reconstruction did not significantly improve the lives of African Americans or even the region as a whole. For nearly a hundred years after the war, the South was one of the poorest regions in the country.

rheumatism—A term sometimes used to describe aches and stiffness in the joints and muscles of older people.

secession—A formal withdrawal from an organization. Eleven Southern States withdrew from the United States, claiming that they had a right to secede because the United States was composed of independent states.

tuberculosis—A disease that can infect any organ of the body, but most often the lungs. Before modern medicine, many people died from tuberculosis.

Union—A term used to identify those who fought to preserve the United States of America. Almost all of the twenty-three Union states were in the North. They included: California, Connecticut, Delaware, Illinois, Indiana, Iowa, Kansas, Kentucky, Maine, Maryland, Massachusetts, Michigan, Minnesota, Missouri, New Hampshire, New Jersey, New York, Ohio, Oregon, Pennsylvania, Rhode Island, Vermont, and Wisconsin. The territories of Colorado, Dakota, Nebraska, Nevada, New Mexico, Utah, and Washington also fought for the Union.

"Yankee"—A nickname for a Union Soldier.

FURTHER READING

Gillis, Jennifer Blizin. *Robert E. Lee: Confederate Commander.* Mankato, Minn.: Compass Point Books, 2005.

King, David C. *The Triangle Histories of the Civil War: Leaders— Robert E. Lee.* Farmington Hills, Minn.: Blackbirch Press, 2001.

McPherson, James M. *Fields of Fury: The American Civil War.* New York: Atheneum Books for Young Readers, 2002.

Murphy, Jim. *The Boy's War.* New York: Clarion Books, 1990.

Rice, Earle, Jr. *Robert E. Lee: First Soldier of the Confederacy.* Greensboro, NC: Morgan Reynolds, 2005.

Robertson, James I, Jr. *Robert E. Lee: Virginian Soldier, American Citizen.* New York: Atheneum Books for Young Readers, 2005.

Stanchak, John. *Eyewitness Civil War.* New York: DK Publishing, 2011.

INDEX